The West

The West

A Sailing Companion to the
West Coast of Scotland

Gigha to Cape Wrath

Ronald Faux

John Bartholomew & Son Limited

First published in Great Britain 1982 by
John Bartholomew and Son Limited,
12 Duncan Street, Edinburgh EH9 1TA

**British Library Cataloguing in Publication
Data**
Faux, Ronald
    The West
    1. Coasts - Scotland   2. Sailing
    I. Title
    914.11'04858   DA 867

    ISBN: 0 7028 8101 5

Printed in Edinburgh
by John Bartholomew & Son Limited.

Acknowledgements

The West is dedicated to the many great friends who have sailed on *Hebe* in patience, good humour and occasional trepidation, as I gathered the material for this book. I am greatly indebted to Joyce Helm for her skilful help with the artwork; to David Burnett, former skipper of *Owl* and a wise west coast hand, for his advice; to Frances, my wife, and Dr Gavin Young for their work on the manuscript; and to Mr Charles Barrington of Seol Alba for his help on the northern section. A special gratitude also to Mr Ronnie Slater of the Royal Ulster Yacht Club without whose timely intervention the project would, literally, have foundered.

The illustrations of the birds and the fish found on the west coast of Scotland are reproduced by kind permission of the Reader's Digest Association Limited, London.

Ronald Faux
Burntisland

Note on the Charts

The charts are intended to be a general guide and I hold no responsibility for their absolute accuracy. The Admiralty does a far better job. They are based on sketch maps with my own observations and soundings calculated to Mean Low Water Springs. True North runs parallel with the edge of the page and soundings are, as soundings should be, in fathoms.

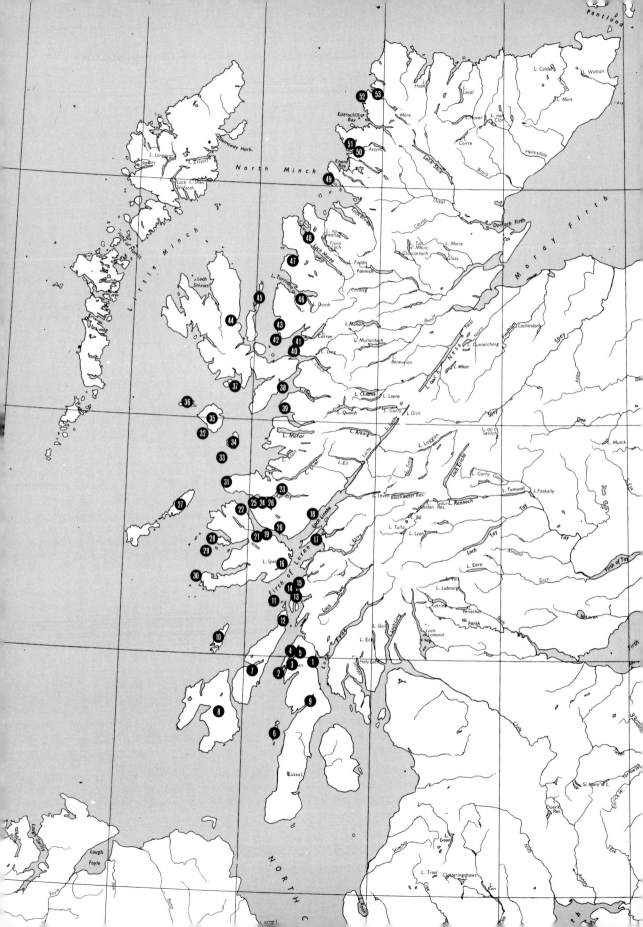

Contents

List of Colour Plates

Introduction

I tried out the idea of a book about 'The West' on a man I knew who mixes a successful business life with his real *raison d'être* of exploring the west coast slowly in an old cutter; the first activity aimed chiefly at supporting the second. He was a sort of weathered tycoon. From the sleeves of his pinstriped jacket there protruded a massive pair of hands, the products of years spent heaving on warps, halyards and anchor chains. He was frankly horrified that anyone should think of producing any book that might possibly make the west coast more popular or better known. 'You must be mad,' he growled at me as if I was a particularly ill wind that had just split his mainsail; 'do you want the place to fill up with people? This is the finest sailing in the world but for heaven's sake don't let the secret out'.

Black-headed Gull. Breeds, often in large colonies, on saltings and coastal lagoons, or on inland marshes and upland bogs; commonly winters inland

The greatest charm of the west coast is that a boat can always nudge its way into a calm patch of water and anchor for the night knowing it will be undisturbed and safe. The boat might arrive in a hurry bucked by a vicious wind over tide that makes the haven all the more attractive to reach, but with a huge length of coastline scattered with hundreds of islands, there is always some islet or headland that throws out a sheltering arm to tuck behind. Compared with the Solent and parts of south-east England the coastline between the Mull of Kintyre and Cape Wrath is virtually undiscovered. The number of boats sailing the West could multiply several times without the slightest threat that the anchorages will become overcrowded or that Tobermory Bay will begin to look like the Hamble. The Clyde Cruising Club *Sailing Directions* detail over 200 anchorages and list hundreds more, so that one yachtsman could spend his whole sailing career here without once entering the same anchorage twice, although that would hardly be conceivable. There are some magical places to which he will return year after year.

It is perfect sailing ground with fine mountains shouldering their way into the water, deep sea lochs wandering miles inland, small ports and communities, a richly varied history and places where a boat gives the only access. Visitors complain about the weather which can be foul when it has a mind, but if the West were bathed throughout the summer in warm sunshine, then the pressure for development would soon give my friend something seriously to complain about.

The West often requires a stoic spirit and a keen appreciation of shades of grey but such bad days are always relieved by times when the sun puts a bright sparkle on the Hebridean sea, when the breeze is steady, the tide is under the stern and sailing among the islands is a delight. In those conditions the islands are unforgettable and most enjoyably explored in a small cruising boat.

This book introduces a selection of anchorages between Gigha and Cape Wrath but is not intended as an alternative to the 'Bible' of west coast sailors, the *Sailing Directions* of the Clyde Cruising Club. That irreplaceable volume remains the key to all west coast exploration simply because of its comprehensive detail and scope. What I hope 'The West' gives is a personal impression of some of the anchorages I was able to sail into during the summer of 1979 when *The Times* was not being published. The charts and illustrations are my own and while I have tried to ensure that they are accurate I hold no responsibility for their accuracy. Much of the sailing was done single-handed in my 21-ft. Snapdragon *Hebe IV,* but I am very grateful to those friends who did join me from time to time to crew *Hebe,* to check depths and to trudge for miles over shore lines and headlands in search of some elusive angle. I hope it will be a helpful companion on board and a prod to memory when the wind howls, the fire roars and all wise owners have their boats decently wintered ashore.

Mackerel

Hebe at anchor at Rudha an Ridire, Sound of Mull

The West Coast

The Outer Hebrides take the weight of the North Atlantic rolling un-
checked from the west. Behind lies a ragged mainland coast some 1,400
miles long if every bay, loch and indent is measured, and a scattering of
some 600 islands. Between stretches the sea of the Hebrides and the sailing
ground of 'The West'. Few coasts have quite such a fine variety of colour,
light and atmosphere; islands that erupt from the sea with tall cliffs alive
with seabirds, islands that lie flat like anchored ships, ribbed with columns
of basalt, and islands that rise in blue-grey mountain ranges. The sea is the
link between these places, a sea that may one day be furrowed by a busy
swell into deep troughs that bury a ferry up to its funnel, or the next lie
limpid and still as a pond.

Heron. Breeds in colonies in
trees; feeds in shallow water
on fish and frogs caught by
stalking at the water's edge

Sailing gives the right pace and perspective for exploring the Inner
Hebrides. Historically the sea was the transport lane along which people
travelled in this region. Apart from the pure pleasure of voyaging between
the harbours described in this book, using the tides and winds judiciously
and avoiding the unmarked sgeirs and shallows, a yachtsman, however
small his craft and limited his skill, can have the satisfaction of arriving at
his port with the feeling that he has also discovered it.

Parts of the West suffered severely under the infamous Clearances in the
nineteenth century, when some Highland lairds replaced people with
more profitable sheep. As a result the region was depopulated and over the
years has become one of the few remaining true wildernesses in Europe.
There are three main segments, beginning with the Mull of Kintyre running north to Ardnamurchan and including the islands of Gigha, Islay,
Jura, Oronsay and Colonsay, the Isles of the Sea and Mull, Coll and Tiree.
Next is the sea area north of Ardnamurchan, the most westerly tip of the
British mainland. There lie the Small Isles and the Isle of Skye with its
own island outriders to the north-east. Finally there is the long stretch of
less protected coastline running from Gairloch to Cape Wrath.

I learned a great deal, mainly through a series of near disasters, in the
years I have spent cruising off the west coast in *Hebe* and on board other
craft. It can be an unforgiving coastline. There are few soft sandbanks and

if a boat runs aground it will more often be onto rocks. There are two rules which have brought me much comfort and which would have saved a deal of danger and embarrassment had I always followed them! The first; always carry an extra anchor and a kedge together with several extra fathoms of chain and warp if possible. The second; always plot your exact course on the chart and run your finger down the line. If your finger hits something, there is a fair chance your boat will follow its example. In other words read the chart extra carefully because in the West you are rarely out of sight of land which makes navigation easier in one respect but harder in others. It is also wise to be well fuelled and victualled since several anchorages lie some distance from the nearest road or the nearest shop.

The beauty of the West is that it offers a rare chance to escape completely from human company or to seek it in the small communities that operate to a quieter time scale. There are strong threads of Gaelic culture running through the islands where, to their cost and credit, the Gaels seem to take life at a deliberately relaxed pace. The story goes of two professors, one Gaelic, the other Spanish, discussing their respective languages. Was there a Gaelic expression for the Spanish term 'manana'? enquired the Spaniard. 'Manana?' repeated the Gael. 'No. In the whole great history of our language there was never felt to be the need for a word that implies such a keen sense of urgency.'

Weather and Tide

If the Outer Isles are invisible across the Minch then you know it is raining. If they are visible you know it will soon be raining. That is one popular way to sum up the weather in the West; the other is to quote a Skye fisherman wise in local forecasting lore who explained the mysteries by reflecting: 'Ah, the weather. It is true to say that on Skye there is a lot of it.' Indeed a local rhyme runs:

> 'Brave would he be of soul who would supply
> A weather forecast for the whole of Skye'

- or for that matter for anywhere along the west coast, because so many influences enter the equation that laying down general rules only invites them to be washed away on a flood of exceptions.

The difficulty is that the coast lies in a lively battleground of elements that conflict and produce a volatile weather pattern. There are the fronts that mature over the North Atlantic and sweep in from the west, sometimes marked by tall anvil-headed cumulo-nimbus clouds that indicate unstable air and the likelihood of strong, gusty winds. The mountainous land of the West often generates very local differences in weather conditions, funnelling the wind when it is in certain directions and brewing cloud when humidity and temperature reach particular levels. It may be helpful to note from the overall weather position where the centre of any depression passes in relation to Scotland as this could influence the subsequent direction of the wind; but if there is a general rule based on the experience of recent summers, it is that the best weather will be had during late May and June whilst the allegedly summer months of July and August can be grim. I vividly remember sitting in the MacDonald Arms in Tobermory watching Wimbledon on television. While Wimbledonians were forced to wear handkerchiefs over their heads to prevent sunstroke and soak up the perspiration, the torrential rain rattled like grapeshot against the windows and out in the bay *Hebe* was straining at her anchor in the sharp gusts. It was winter cold and miserably wet but, as the person manning the tourist office observed, it kept the midges down.

The previous day in Oban I had studied the impressive-looking barometer in the entrance to the Caledonian Hotel which was forecasting fair weather. So, too, were the weathermen and at Oban Coastguard Station the officer on duty had predicted a fine spell even though his words were pretty well drowned by the drumming of rain on the roof of his hut. Weather prophets have a thankless time on the west coast of Scotland when isobars may suddenly bunch themselves together into a sold line sending the barometric pressure plummeting and the wind force soaring.

Good signs for approaching settled weather include the adage of a red sky at night and an evening rainbow if the wind is in the west. 'With a mackerel sky let your royals fly' is sound advice to yachtsmen and on the West the caveat 'But with mare's tails close reef your sails' holds equally well. High, wispy cirrus clouds streaming from the Atlantic invariably herald the leading edge of a depression or frontal system. If the cirrus thickens and lowers to become cirrostratus, this is added confirmation the bad weather could be on its way.

Oystercatcher. Noisy wader which breeds on shores and sometimes in river valleys; feeds on shellfish and marine worms

A chart of average wind directions in Skye taken over a 12-year period shows that during May, the wind blew out of the south and west on 16 days and out of the north and east nearly 15 days. In June the respective average was 17 and 12 days; July, 16 and 14; August, 16 and 15. I mention this to suggest the wisdom of allowing the wind to dictate which direction to head in rather than sticking rigidly to some predetermined plot. I may have been unlucky but whenever I have decided to press on regardless into the prevailing wind direction, it has invariably meant a beat all the way there and an equally arduous thrash back, while the simple rule of using the wind to your swiftest advantage always adds a spice of uncertainty about where the night's anchorage might be; the fleshpots of Craignure perhaps or the solitude of the Garvellochs.

What applies to the wind goes equally for the tide which is a powerful ally off the West and a stubborn, sometimes impassable opponent. Tidal streams that sweep along the coast develop formidable strength when they are forced into the labyrinth of channels between the Inner Hebrides. Some are notoriously dangerous. The Gulf of Corryvreckan between the islands of Jura and Scarba is surely the worst, where the spring tide sets through the channel at 8 knots and severe turbulence is caused even in moderate west winds. When winter and storms are added to the confusion the resulting roar can be heard miles away. A little further north between Scarba and Lunga lies the Little Corryvreckan or the Grey Dogs, where the tide runs like a mill race on either side of Bheallaigh Island. For the rest the channels of the West provide exhilarating sailing provided the tide is used as an aid and a careful eye is kept on the wind conditions which may build up a short and difficult sea.

Places where careful timing is essential are Cuan Sound, a narrow dog's leg between Seil, Luing and Torsa, where a yacht may only sail with the tide and where all on board may receive the strong impression that they are sailing downhill. Kyle Rhea which links the Sound of Sleat with Loch Alsh has an 8-knot southerly ebb that may be difficult when a strong south westerly blows against the narrow opening of the channel when the tide is ebbing out.

At many points along the west coast, even in calm weather, the sea will suddenly and mysteriously begin to swirl and bubble as a million or more tons of water come to a halt and gather momentum in a new direction.

A broad picture of the tidal movements begins with an east-bound flood arriving along the north coast of Ireland. At the North Channel it divides. The southern stream heads for the Irish Sea, a central branch washes round the Mull of Kintyre into the Clyde estuary and a north-bound stream flows up the Kintyre coast passing Gigha into the Sound of Jura and Firth of Lorne, filling the lochs on its way. Another stream sweeps both east and west of Islay and joins the main north-east-bound flood which runs as far north as the Little Minch.

The flood tide moves eastwards along the south-east coast of Mull to join the waters flooding up the Sound of Jura. In the principal east-west channels of the Dorus Mor, the Corryvreckan, the Grey Dogs, Cuan Sound and Easdale Sound the flood runs west. The stream runs north through Iona and Ulva Sounds and up the west coast of Mull. In the Sound of Mull the flood runs north-west and divides east into Loch Sunart and west towards Ardnamurchan Point. Between Muck and Eigg, Coll and Tiree the tide floods north-west. In the Sound of Sleat and into Kyle Rhea the flood runs north. In Loch Alsh and past Kyle it flows west along the Skye coast until it reaches the Raasay Narrows.

The tidal anomaly at the Raasay Narrows is confusing if it is met unexpectedly. The direction changes, the flood setting southwards and the ebb northwards at between 2 and 3 knots. The flood starts ¼ hr. after L.W. and runs 5 hours. Constant: -4.33 Dover. The ebb begins ¾ hr. before H.W. and runs for 7 hours.

In Scalpay Sound the flood runs north-west but in Caol Mor, between Scalpay and Raasay, the weight of water flooding from the north takes precedence and the flood is south-bound. In Lochs Carron and Kishorn, it turns eastwards. Down the Inner Sound the flood is southwards as far as the Crowlin Islands.

North of Skye the flood tide flows north to the Butt of Lewis and swings eastwards across the Minch to flow northwards to Cape Wrath. It is worth noting that the tide floods into all the lochs and bays except the north entrances to Oban and Tobermory where it flows outwards. In effect, the ebb runs in direct reverse to the flood, but it is recommended that anyone exploring the West should invest in the Admiralty Tidal Stream Atlas, North Coast of Ireland and West Coast of Scotland (NP 218).

The Anchorages

ARDRISHAIG AND CRINAN

Map ref. 4A5, 4B6
All facilities available

The best gateway to the West is undoubtedly the Crinan Canal which cuts across the long Kintyre peninsula at a narrow point between Ardrishaig and Crinan. It is a delightful waterway, tree-sheltered, narrow and always interesting. It curves gently through countryside parallel to the road for 9 miles and saves the strenuous 80 miles passage round the Mull of Kintyre, important in the days when sails powered the working vessels which were numerous along this coast.

Work on building the canal began in 1794 after the Act had been passed the previous year authorising the project. The survey and estimates were done by Sir John Rennie for a company of gentlemen headed by the Duke of Argyll. Unfortunately the scheme from the start was under-capitalised and continually suffered from cash shortage. It was first opened in July 1801 in an unfinished state but had to be closed four years later

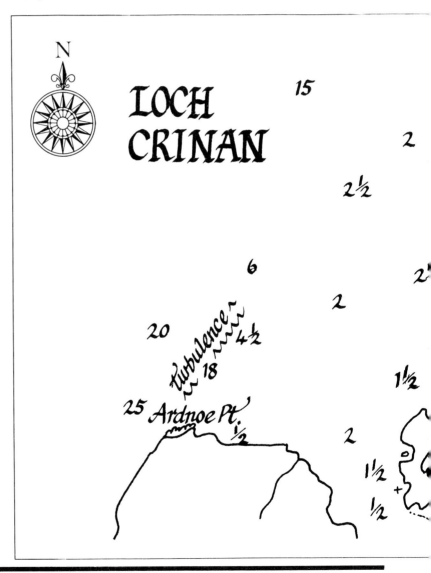

when 70 yards of canal bank were destroyed by flooding. The reopening was in 1809 and the waterway flowed gently on until 1816 when Thomas Telford, builder of the Caledonian Canal, inspected the Crinan waterway and drew up a list of significant defects. Not until November 1817 was the canal brought to a satisfactory state. The growth of larger steam vessels meant a decline in importance of the canal among commercial shipping but the increase in the number of pleasure craft passing between the Clyde and the Hebrides ensured brisk business throughout the spring, summer and autumn.

Long pleasant reaches separate the flights of locks and the Cairnbaan Hotel lies beside the canal at about half-way mark. Vessels may spend one night in the canal although the whole passage may take as little as 4½ hours to complete. It is smartly maintained but has largely become a do-it-

Shelduck. Breeds in burrows on low-lying sandy coasts; feeds on minute marine life. Migrates annually to moult

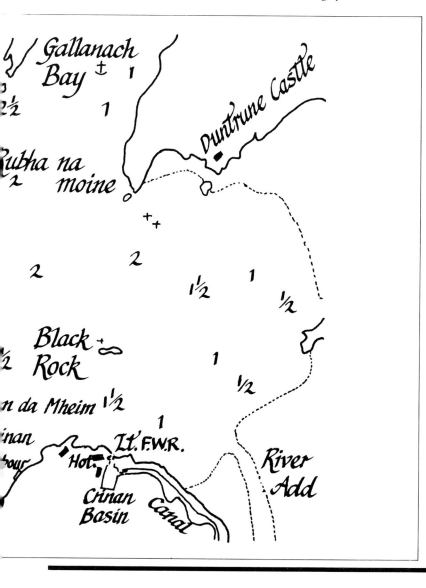

yourself canal with small flotillas of yachts helping one another through the groups of 15 locks which lift them over the 64ft. hump of countryside between Loch Fyne and the Crinan sea lock from where the wind will tilt their masts, billow their sails and scatter them among the Hebrides.

We arrived off Ardrishaig breakwater the previous evening, led there by a white light flashing every six seconds. It had been a long sail in one day from Gourock through the Kyles of Bute, but we were anxious to reach the West.

We spent the night comfortably just off the sea lock gates sleeping the sleep of the well-voyaged yachtsman and when the canal office near the pier opened the next day, I picked up the papers and ticket. The sea lock gate ground open and *Hebe* was soon spluttering into a crowded basin.

'I say, would you care to join our group - then we can sort of help one another through?' asked a polite character in a plastic tub about the size of my own. In the group was a motor yacht with a tall flying bridge operated by two friends in white duck, navy-blue blazers and silk cravats. There was one other small craft and a solid-looking wooden ketch with a stern like a bustle.

Whiting

There had already been a bit of furore in the first lock above the basin. The keeper, a man with expressionless features who had seen most kinds of marine misery, had peered into the shadows at the bottom of the lock from where had come a shrill scream, the roar of a diesel engine being thrust into reverse and the awful sound of an impact. He had winced, as the owner of a china shop might wince upon the entry of a bull. An amateur Commodore in a broad-beamed gin palace had jumbled his forward with his astern and had charged the gate in spirited style. It brought the row of retired seafarers who wait near the canal on sunny mornings to their feet. There would be another bruise on the old woodwork, a reminder that Scottish canals are no longer commercial arteries and that not all modern skippers have the skill to manoeuvre their vessels to within an old-fashioned sixpence width of the lock gates.

'Do nothing', the lock-keeper boomed into the depths, 'except throw me a rope'. It was a minor scrape, a run-of-the-lock scare. He recalled other craft mounting one another in the locks as though they were trying to breed. Another vessel actually sank while the two men on board, well influenced by the essence of the West, argued whether the tree to which they should have tied it was an oak or an elm.

It took us about three or four locks before we had the hang of navigating the canal, after which ropes were snaking up from the depths with deft precision, water levels were altered with aplomb and the passage became pure pleasure. There is no limit on mast height and the Crinan will take vessels up to 80ft. long, 20ft in beam and drawing 12ft. After about three hours we had reached the Cairnbaan Hotel. It was a beautiful day; lock-opening was thirsty work so we tied up for a drop of lunch.

It was about this time of year in 1847 that Queen Victoria sailed along the canal in a magnificently decorated barge drawn by three horses ridden by postilions in scarlet. Since then a large variety of boats have sailed across Kintyre from the ubiquitous Clyde 'puffers' to wartime midget submarines. There have been paddle steamers and barges, pleasure craft and hovercraft. From Bellanoch Lagoon, a delightful place to stop, a last long reach winds westwards and eventually the canal runs above the estuary of the River Add beyond which lie the stone walls of Duntroon Castle. A flight of locks lead down into the Crinan Basin which may hold more than £1m. worth of yachts in the busy season waiting to get into the sea lock or else waiting to begin the eastwards passage of the canal; sleek, costly yachts and launches that contrast oddly with the battered-looking workboats used to harvest clams, lobsters and other shellfish.

We enjoyed a seafood meal of langouste with a bottle of fine dry white wine at the Crinan Hotel and watched the sun set over Jura and the Dorus Mor (the Great Door). It was the end of a perfect day with another one forecast to follow. The night was warm, the forest of masts rooted in raft upon raft of yachts barely stirred and the brown water of the basin lay still.

There was no rush the next day. We decided to obey the rule of following the wind, which blew steadily from the north-west. That meant heading down the Sound of Jura and catching the tide from Crinan at high water, still a few hours ahead. Even so we joined a pack of yachts in the sea lock, sinking into the cool gloom between black slime walls as the level lowered and the fresh water from the canal rushed into the sea. Creaking and straining the lock gates swung open and there lay the West. It is always worth going through the Crinan Canal for that moment alone, moving out from the dark confines of the lock into some 30,000 square miles of superb sailing water with the Dorus Mor ahead off Craignish Point and a 7-knot tide flowing through it.

Hebe motored from the canal entrance round to the harbour where we tied up for lunch. It is best to borrow a mooring here if possible on account of the permanent mooring chains that lie on the harbour floor to which my own anchor flies with the attraction of a powerful magnet. Trevor uncorked the bottle of Bull's Blood to allow it to breathe and reach cockpit temperature and we waited for the water to lap gently up the old stonework of the quay. The harbour, which is a very popular yacht mooring, was quite crowded. We saw the doughty *VIC 32,* last of the steam powered 'puffers', setting out from Crinan on a cruise.

Soon, only a few steps remained dry and the tide was approaching slack water. We slipped the mooring and motored out to Ardnoe Point. After a turn south-west, the main and genoa were set. The engine died and was hoisted into its small compartment astern; *Hebe* settled on a steady broad reach down the Sound of Jura. Immediately north lay Loch Craignish which is well worth exploring and provides an alternative anchorage in which to wait for the tide. The islands beside the north-west shore give good shelter and at Ardfern there is a chandlery, proper moorings and the Galley of Lorne Hotel which serves excellent seafood. This was a favourite cruising ground for the west coast steamers, gliding down the deep narrow channel between Eilean Righ and the mainland past quiet bays that are still superintended by the occasional prosperous-looking heron standing motionless at the water's edge (chart page 40).

MacCORMAIG ISLES

Map ref. 2D1
Water (well, Eilean Mor);
avoid in northerlies

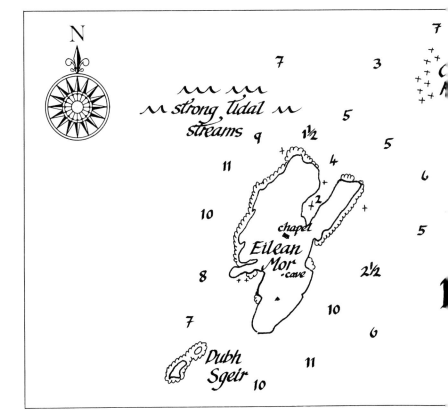

The laird of these small, bare islands is the Scottish National Party, not that St. Cormac showed any other affiliations than to prayer and an austere life. From the north the main island of Eilean Mor is guarded by the Cor Rocks and some unpleasantly shoal water. I remembered the first time I had tried to land there with a westerly gale blowing across the flood

Eilean Mor on the MacCormaig Isles; the ruins of St Cormac's chapel lie in the foreground

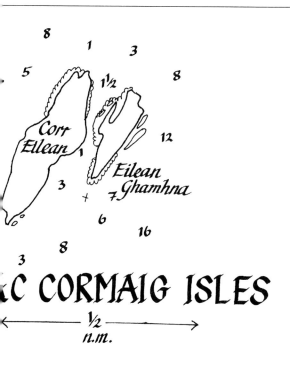

8
1   3
5   8
1½
Corr
Eilean   12
3
Eilean
Ghamhna
+   7
6
16
3   8
3

C CORMAIG ISLES

←——————— ½ ——————→
n.m.

tide. We bore away from the seas that were exploding around the islands, chased by huge rolling waves. It was too wild to risk a jibe into Loch Sween so we beat into the shelter of Eilean nan Leac, did our turn there, and then came out into the gale again, racing for the shelter of the loch.

Today the seas were calm and sparkling and the deep gut in the north-east of Eilean Mor was an unrippled pool. The sailing directions warn of rocks west of the entrance and a solitary rock near the head of the small bay. Several yachtsmen I have spoken to all give different locations for this obstacle and one claimed to have it in a position it was not supposed to be. Perhaps the unsaintly spirit of Cormac is rolling it mischievously about the bed of the bay. There are the remains of his chapel, easily seen from the anchorage, and a cross on the highest point of the island from which the view is superb. At a lower level you will find St. Cormac's cave, a deep, extremely damp grotto which was used as a retreat within a reatreat when the monk felt the need for even greater austerity. It is characteristic of the Celtic Church and on the walls are two inscribed crosses dating back to the eighth century. The veneration of this place continued after the Saint had been laid in his tomb near the chapel and a second chapel was built near the cave mouth. The ruins remain. We merely sailed in, keeping to the eastern edge of the gut and then eased away from the shore past an outcrop of quartz which marks a submerged reef coming out from the east shore. Two red marks on the western shore come into line above the alleged rock. We sailed slightly beyond and anchored in 10ft.

Common Sandpiper. Nests in sheltered hollows near gravelly or rocky rivers and beside lakes

LOCH SWEEN

Map ref. 4A6

The wind backed further north and the afternoon forecast was for it to remain in the same direction but increase in strength. The memory of the MacCormaigs surrounded by white water and the exposure of the anchorage to winds from the north persuaded us to up-anchor before we had a chance to pinpoint the mysterious rock by driving on it. We motored out and turned sharply towards Corr Eilean, leaving the shallow patch to port and heading for the southern edge of Danna Island, now clear and golden in the evening light. It was a delightful broad reach to the mouth of the loch where we caught the north-bound tide and by leaving the group of rocks at the western entrance to the loch close to port, *Hebe* was just able to make the imposing ruin of Castle Sween in one fetch.

It was clear why this twelfth-century fortress was of commanding local importance since it overlooks the mouth of the loch which was once a busy sea route. Indeed it may date back to the late eleventh century, making it the oldest medieval stone fortress in Scotland, and was most likely built by the Normans. Traditionally it was thought to have been built by Swein, prince of Denmark, but that has been discounted. It had a stormy history. Robert the Bruce besieged Alexander of the Isles here and later imprisoned him in Dundonald Castle. The Royalists reduced Castle Sween to a ruin during the Civil War. Now its tall grey walls appear to be under siege from an army of caravans.

The wind confounded the forecast and died altogether. The waters of the loch edged themselves with hardly a ripple towards the wooded headland round which lies the near-perfect anchorage of Tayvallich. It was completely dark as *Hebe* felt her way through the rock spit guarding the entrance. A colony of guillemots chattered at us as in the gloom we headed for the lights of the hotel, drifting over a line of submerged rocks, we later discovered. We marvelled at our luck - not at missing the rocks but at finding a pub where the usually infallible *Sailing Directions* mark only a petrol pump.

The reef guarding the entrance to Tayvallich harbour, Loch Sween

Although there is little chance of swell reaching a yacht anchored here, the high hills surrounding the bay generate some powerful gusts of wind. Enter by leaving the end of the rock finger to port and turn 90 degrees towards the western end of the pool which has a reef extending for about 2 cables half way across it and running SW - NE. Sail along the northern edge of the rock finger until an obvious rock face is reached. It is then clear to turn into the inner pool. There are a number of small jetties and a crumbling pier at which it is possible to tie up. This is occasionally used by fishing boats. Tayvallich has a Post Office, and a general store in the small tin building. Outside there is a tap. The Tayvallich Inn has an excellent restaurant serving *moules marinières* which are superb. The wine is good, the service friendly and the moules, 'grown' locally in Caol Scotnish, are delivered daily by 'Phil the Muscle'.

TAYVALLICH

Map ref. 4A6
Water (taps), inn, shop, PO

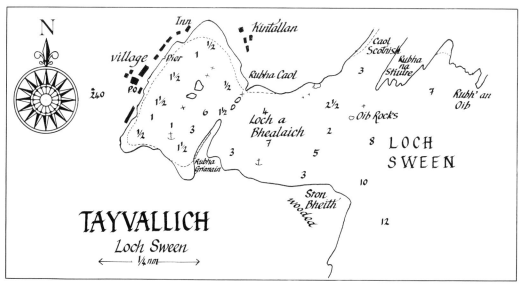

Fir-lined calm in the Fairy Isles, Loch Sween

THE FAIRY ISLES

Map ref. 4A6
No facilities

The wind backed and strengthened to a full gale the next day, whipping a short, nasty sea out in the loch but leaving Tayvallich pool almost unruffl-ed. We ventured out with the smallest jib and much of the mainsail wound on to the boom. Immediately we were clear of Sron Bheith, the high wooded headland, *Hebe* reeled under the blast blowing up the loch. We bore away on a swift run for about ¾ mile until a series of long, low islets lay abeam. With the main dropped we swept through into a delec-table, beautifully protected pool known as the Fairy Isles. Absolute pro-tection for bilge keelers may be had by drying out on the mud bed further inland, a completely quiet and isolated sanctuary. Isolation is paid for, of course, by complete absence of any facilities and with the Tayvallich Inn and the Crinan Hotel so near it would test the abstinence of a Saint Cor-mac to stay there too long. The rain lashed down, the wind on the other side of Sgeir Bhuide, the Fairy Isle dividing the pool from the loch, howl-ed mournfully and rattled the shrouds on *Hebe*. In the cabin, the warmth of the cooker heated both the evening meal and my spirits. A bottle of Bull's Blood was fished from the locker and long before the 00.15 forecast and the nightly recital of 'Sailing By' I was sound asleep.

The next morning a heron was watching me from shore, standing still and elegant. The sky was still overcast and the wind had a chilled edge to it.

right A summer's day on the Crinan Canal
over The Fairy Isles off Loch Sween afford wooded protection

This part of the peninsula which ends at the Mull of Kintyre is known as Knapdale and is solid forest. Fifty years ago it was either bog or semi-derelict farmland but now the Forestry Commission has transformed the area with a fresh covering of woodland of almost 9,000 acres. The main species is the ubiquitous sitka spruce but there is also a sprinkling of oak, ash, rowan, birch, alder, hazel and willow. It was not a day to be heading out to open water with gales for Malin and Hebrides being forecast. We tacked south for a mile to clear Rubha na Marraidh and enter the easterly arm of Loch Sween that leads up to Achnamara where the shore by the village was nicely sheltered. From here there are some good forest walks and since we had been confined to the boat for some 24 hours it was good to stretch our legs. Near the anchorage was a clapper bridge over a stream with drystone piers and a decking of two large stones. It was built in the seventeenth century as a penance for non-attendance at church. The walks from Achnamara cover a short route of a mile and a longer one of 2½ miles which climbs onto high ground that gives some fine views.

From my corner of Tayvallich the evening sky has taken on the deep red hue delightful to sailors. It turns the pool into gold and burnishes the mast of the boat anchored next to *Hebe*. The wind has changed with the tide which now has the upper hand and swings everyone into a new position with the precision of a corps de ballet. Tomorrow will be fine at last and no longer will there be the ceaseless slap of halyards and a cool bite to the wind. From a heavy black cutter with tan sails that lumbered in earlier this evening comes a drift of Chopin's music. All the crew must be drawing their pensions but none could be enjoying themselves more. They are all clambering into a dinghy, no doubt bound for the *moules marinières*. I think I will join them.

The gardener working near the grounds of Achamore House was totally bewildered. Spring and early summer had arrived during the same week after the most prolonged winter he could remember. Now snowdrops and tulips were thrusting their way out of the ground along with daffodils and the first burst of blossom from the rhododendrons. Gigha's fertile earth was suddenly unlocked by a superb spell of warm weather that turned the sea around 'God's Isle' a translucent blue but sadly robbed the skies of wind.

Hebe's arrival the previous evening had not been at all salubrious. We had motored down the east coast of the island which fairly bristles with reefs and anchored in Druimyeon Bay. It was calm weather; what little breeze there was stirred in from the west leaving the lee side of the island like a millpond at high water. We decided to try the next bay down as the final anchorage of the day and with infinite care navigated *Hebe* through the shoals of Druimyeon and around the rock island that ends in Ardminish Point. The large chart, which I did not have, marks a reef that projects due south from that island and ends in a prominent rock which dries at low water. It could have been the broad open aspect of Ardminish Bay, the smoke curling up from the houses and the warm lights of the

GIGHA

Map ref. 2D3
Water (tap and well), hotel, shop, PO

left The fine shelter of Tobermory Bay

Gigha Hotel that distracted me. There is really no excuse; with a spine-chilling thud *Hebe's* starboard keel struck rock; the boat abruptly stopped, burying its bow. On a descending tide, in what one glance over the side revealed as rock-bottomed shallows, I was in a vulnerable position. I had put out two kedges into deep water and was ready to try and winch myself off when the launch used as the Gigha ferry inched towards me and took a line. She had to pull from astern which took some splinters of glass fibre out of my rudder skeg. I was soon afloat again, heart thumping, the boat a chaos of rope, chain and seaweed. I cursed my incompetence. 'Don't worry,' the boatsman called philosophically, 'you're not the first and you won't be the last to land there'. The ferry chugged away towards the pier and I followed to put down the anchor in 1 fathom off the pier. I sorted out the mess, cooked a meal and tried to calm down. The proper way to enter Ardminish, which is a deceptively open bay, is to keep well offshore until two quite identical cottages on the shore come into line. Only at that point head inshore, missing the rocks that lie on both sides of this entrance line. A third anchorage useful in bad weather or when the wind is in the east lies between the southern tip of Gigha and Gigulum Island.

Gigha

The open sweep of Ardminish Bay, Gigha

Gigha itself is one of the most beautiful islands in the Hebrides and quite unlike its bare, austere neighbours. The ground is fertile, the grounds of Sir James Horlick's home at Achamore House are superb with a rich variety of plants and the broad shelter belts of trees give a distinctly un-Hebridean look to the island. The hotel at Ardminish is highly recommended for its standard of comfort and cuisine and the willingness of its proprietor to rescue wayward yachtsmen from the reefs of Ardminish.

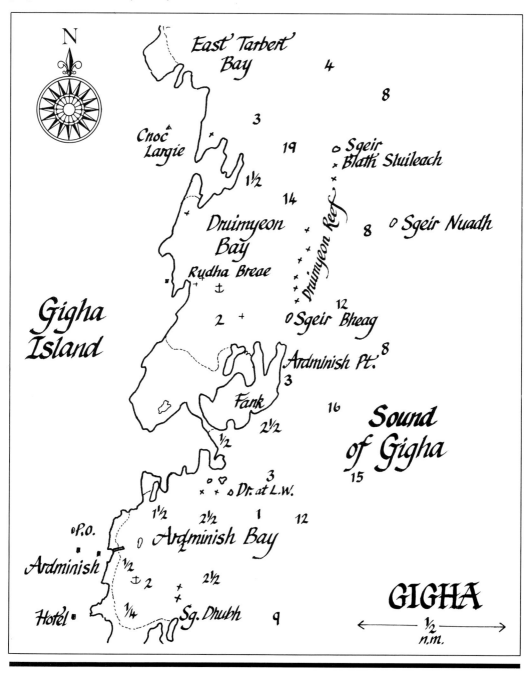

N

East Tarbert Bay

4

8

3

Cnoc Largie

19

Sgeir Blath Sluileach

1½

14

Druimyeon Bay

Druimyeon Reef

8

Sgeir Nuadh

Rudha Breae

Gigha Island

2

12

Sgeir Bheag

Ardminish Pt.

8

3

Fank

16

Sound of Gigha

2½

½

15

3

Dr. at L.W.

1½

2½

1

12

P.O.

Ardminish Bay

Ardminish

½

2

2½

Hotel

¼

Sg. Dhubh

9

GIGHA

½
n.m.

JURA

Map ref. 2C1
Water (by pier), hotel,
shop, PO

From the lonely light of Skervuile with its dark rock made even darker by the bodies of slumbering seals, there was a choice of courses. Either we could head south-west towards Craighouse and the Small Isles or visit the broad loop of Lowlandman's Bay. It was fine weather, the Paps of Jura made a graceful backdrop to the sea and there was just enough wind to fill the sails efficiently. *Hebe* reached around the red and white ringed buoy marking a 9 ft. rock and ran smoothly through the mouth of the Bay. We stayed only a short time but the holding ground was poor, perhaps because with the boat's shallow draught I had got too close in to the jetty. The anchor lay jammed among a mass of boulders. The wind died during the meal and we had to motor from the Bay down around the rocks off An Dunan and in behind the Small Isles.

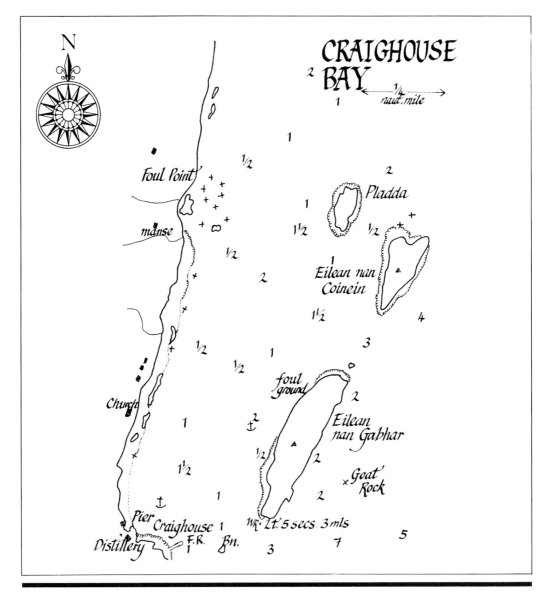

'There may not look as if there is life on Jura but you can reckon there were a score or more glasses observing your approach,' a fisherman at the old harbour told me. I tied up there because I wanted *Hebe* to dry out so that I could inspect her for any signs of deeper damage after our brush with the rocks on Gigha. There is another modern pier used by steamers but that appeared to be in quite a bit of swell.

Ideally I would have preferred the anchorage tucked in the shelter of Eilean nan Gabhar, the largest and southernmost of the Small Isles. The tide retreated, *Hebe* settled on her keels and a close inspection showed no more damage than a few lumps of fibreglass chipped from the leading edge. That night I slept soundly.

Jura is a large island, rightly known as the Isle of Deer since there are some 200 people and 5,000 red deer inhabiting it. With the Corryvreckan above and the Sound of Islay below, it is swept by some powerful tides but the anchorages on the east side are well protected. It is an island of emptiness with most of its 28 miles by 8 miles divided up into sporting estates. The Vikings were here once but its proximity to Iona brought a strong Christian influence. Latterly George Orwell lived here between 1946-48 in a croft on the northern tip of the island where he wrote *1984*.

It is wise to clear any wanderings off the beaten track with the chief stalker during the shooting season which for stags runs from mid-August to mid-October. Hinds are shot from November to February and do not usually clash with wandering sailors. The records in the small, neat church at Kilearnadil reflect the toll that wars and the sea have taken of the community when the island had a much larger population. One cemetery marks the burial place of Mary MacCrain who died in 1856, aged 128, a descendant of Gillour MacCrain, who kept 108 Christmases in his own house and who died in the reign of Charles I.

They are long-lived on Jura with their quiet way of life. One farmer I met still kept a family diary in Gaelic begun by his forefathers 300 years ago. Craighouse has a comfortable hotel where a yachtsman, like some migrating bird seeking somewhere to land, may find a bath. There is a licensed general store behind the old pier and a rather austere-looking distillery.

Raised beaches at Loch Tarbert, Jura

ISLAY

Map ref. 2B2
Port Askaig: water (at pier),
hotel, shop, PO

We slipped into the Sound of Islay with the tail-end of the north-bound tide behind us. 'A good place to see fishing boats moving along like lorries down a motorway,' one local had remarked. It was a relatively gentle tide today, the sea surface still and the sails hanging limply. I turned on the motor to keep us well clear of Am Fraoch Eilean - where MacDonald of the Isles kept his prisoners in Castle Cluig - and the rocks beyond. Port Askaig lay 4 miles further up the sound and since the tide was due to turn as we reached there, we tied up.

Islay could hardly be more different from its near neighbour Jura. It is fertile and with 500 farms is intensively cultivated even though much of the landmass is trackless peat bog providing the water that is the essential and subtle ingredient for the eight distilleries sited here. Islay is renowned for its malt whisky-making which dates back to the 1770s. One calculation is that the industry's earnings now represent some £1m. a year for each distillery worker on the island.

It has a long and rich history. For some 300 years it was part of the Scots kingdom of Dalriada until with the rest of the Western Isles it fell under Norse rule from about 850 to 1150. Then a sea battle off Islay in which Somerled, king of Argyll, defeated his brother-in-law Godred, Norse King of the Isles, led to the Norwegians being driven out of the southern Hebrides. Somerled settled in Islay and founded the Clan Donald, named for his grandson Donald of Islay, which became immensely powerful. It was Donald's great-grandson, John, who took the title Lord of the Isles. He ruled the Hebrides from Islay with strong autonomy, making treaties with England, France and Ireland.

There are still reminders of this period in Islay's history. Lagavulin Bay is overlooked by the ruins of Dunyvaig Castle, a twelfth - century stronghold of the Lords of the Isles, and the bay itself was where the war-galleys of the Macdonalds anchored. The birdlife on Islay is particularly rich with more than 200 varieties recorded. More than half that number breed on the island and Laggan Bay is a favourite wintering ground for barnacle geese. Choughs, rare in Britain, are comparatively common at the Oa, west of Port Ellen.

Port Askaig is a delightful little harbour. Parts of the hotel, set amongst trees by the water's edge, date back to the sixteenth century. From here a ferry fights the tides across to Feolin on Jura. There is enough water for a small yacht to lie afloat against the north wall but there is better holding ground opposite Caol Isla Distillery a little further north. It is possible to arrange transport around the island from Port Askaig.

The tide returned to a north-bound stream and *Hebe* needed a strong blast of power to turn her steadily into the stream so that she could free-wheel northwards keeping mid-channel past Rudha a Mhail on the tip of Islay. The forecast was set fair with a continuing anticyclone and light winds so we decided to explore one of the wildest and most remote anchorages, Loch Tarbert, Jura.

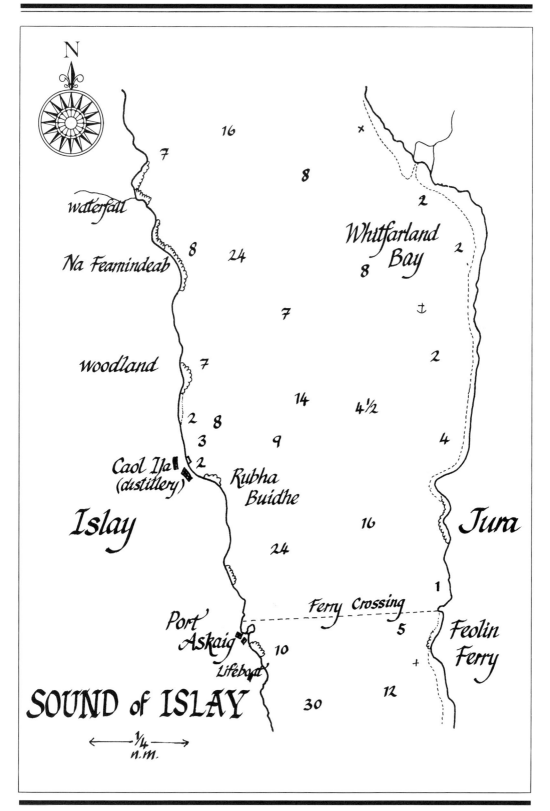

N

16

7

8

2

waterfall

Whitfarland
Bay

2

2

8

24

8

Na Feamindeab

7

7

2

woodland

7

14

4½

4

2

8

3

9

2

16

Caol Ila
(distillery)

Rubha
Buidhe

Islay

Jura

24

16

1

Ferry Crossing

Port
Askaig

5

Feolin
Ferry

10

Lifeboat

+

SOUND of ISLAY

12

30

¼
n.m.

LOCH TARBERT

Map ref. 7D8
No facilities

The loch almost severs Jura into two halves and is well studded with reefs. In strong west winds it is not to be recommended as a bad swell is said to develop which makes navigation amongst the numerous rocks and shoals a hazardous business. We took the southerly dog's leg around Sgeiran Bhudregain and its outriding rocks, missed the buoy marking the safe passage into the loch but lined up the two beacons on the southern shore which served to point the course to Gunhawn Mor on the opposite shore. The anchorage was snug, deserted and quite perfect. I could see the anchor snake down into 20 ft. of water and bite into the sand. *Hebe* swung round and lay to the tide just as a magnificent sunset burnished the sky and turned Beinn an Oir, the highest of the Paps of Jura, into a pyramid of gold.

On both shores of Loch Tarbert there are raised beaches of white quartzite shingle, formed perhaps 10,000 years ago when the huge burden of the Ice Age melted and the land gradually rose above sea level. The beaches in Loch Tarbert are the most remarkable examples in Scotland.

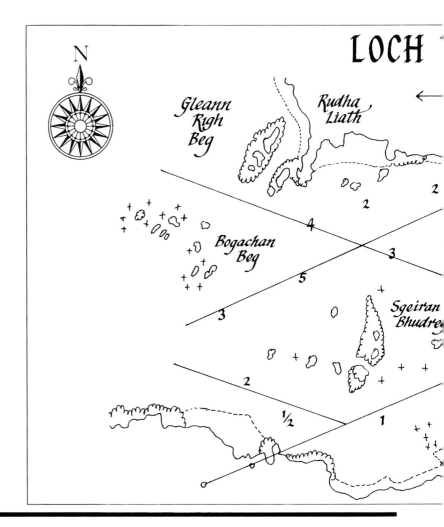

They look exactly what they are; sea shores that have deserted the sea and now lie as much as 100 ft. above water level.

I took ashore two mackerel caught on a spinner and a bottle of Bull's Blood. A fire made of driftwood was soon brighter than the dying sun. The mackerel sizzled, the sea rustled against the shingle and beyond the firelight a few gulls grumbled to one another.

The next day was hot from the start with still air and the loch surface glassy. *Hebe* crossed to the south shore and picked her way through the reefs to anchor off the shooting lodge in Glenbatrick. Less than two hours later I was on the top of Beinn an Oir with a fine view down into the loch where *Hebe* lay, a tiny white speck. Jura was baking hot and tinder dry. The moorland looked as if it had been specially groomed to support deer and the boat was the only man-made object to pick out. The mouth of the loch was wide with the wild western coast of Jura opening out on both sides. A few miles north of the entrance lies Corpach Bay or the Bay of Corpses. It was the custom to leave the bodies of the dead here until the winter storms had passed and they could be taken for burial on Iona.

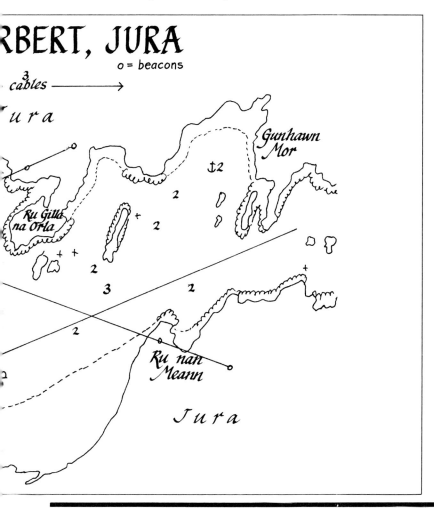

COLONSAY

Map ref. 7C8
Water (well), hotel,
shop, PO; avoid
in easterlies

It took one morning's broad reach to cover the distance from Loch Tarbert to Colonsay; a fast fresh sail that only slowed when the east coast of the island sheltered *Hebe* in its lee. There is a clear passage along the shore south of Scalasaig where we slipped beneath the conspicuous memorial and in well towards the entrance of the inner harbour (which dries out). The anchor bit into sand and in about a fathom of water. Bigger boats are advised to use a ring in the rock on the southern shore with one or more anchors to shelter close in, avoiding the frequent swell that rolls past the island, and to restrict swinging in an often crowded anchorage. The stout pier is used regularly by Caledonian MacBrayne steamers and fishing boats spend the night there. We watched *VIC 32* approaching beneath an authentic black plume of smoke with a piper in the bow playing 'The Skye Boat Song'. Whether this was a shortage of repertoire or a navigational error we never found out. Two passengers had tear-stained cheeks; whether this was coal fumes or emotion we never found out either.

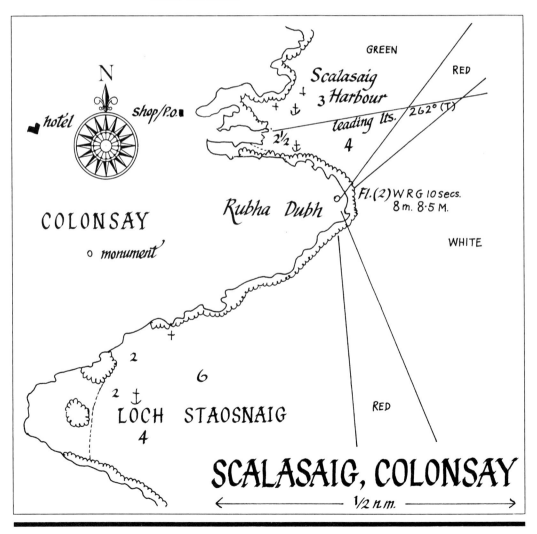

SCALASAIG, COLONSAY

← ½ n.m. →

Colonsay has a good hotel that hires bicycles on which to explore the island. Colonsay House, home of Lord Strathcona, has sub-tropical gardens and there are superb sands at Kiloran Bay on the west side of the island which has a first class alternative anchorage at Port Mhor when the wind is in the east. Further exploration of the west coast is not advised. Its rugged cliffs are breeding grounds for kittiwakes, guillemots and razor-bills.

'Puffer' at Scalasaig, Colonsay

The island is a complete contrast with Jura, rich in archaeological remains and bird life; the eider is known locally as the Colonsay duck. There is an airstrip, and the day we arrived two shaken aviators were waiting to travel home by boat after their light aircraft had caught a wheel in a rabbit hole whilst landing and turned turtle.

The island is owned by Lord Strathcona, formerly a government minister, who is easing the economy towards self-catering tourism. Scalasaig has a Post Office, public telephone, grocer, and water at the Well of the South Wind beyond the pier. Fishermen and masters of trading vessels used to visit it and leave offerings and pray for a south wind. The well is now a cool repository on hot days for cartons of milk.

At low tide Colonsay is linked with the small island of Oronsay by a broad strand which disappears when the tide floods over it. Early on a still morning we left Scalasaig and slipped down the east coast of the island. The sea was still and hung with mist, the water swilling over the shallow divide between the two islands. We took a broad semi-circle around the tip of Eilean-Traig-Naish and its scattering of reefs into the quiet pool behind the rocks.

Oronsay is a flat island edged with machair and a favourite haunt of seals. It is a well-known wintering ground for barnacle geese. Both islands were once leading religious centres with a dozen churches, principal among them Oronsay Priory dating back to the fourteenth century. This is the largest surviving monastic building, after Iona, in the Western Isles. It was built about 1360 by John of Islay on the site of a sixth-century monastery. The rich and the powerful were buried here and there is some superb stonework to be seen including 30 carved grave slabs and a tall celtic cross. One crevice behind the cloisters contained a cache of human bones.

GARVELLOCH ISLANDS

Map ref. 7E6
Water (spring near chapel)

It was late evening when we arrived off the Isles of the Sea, the more romantic name for the Garvellochs. *Hebe* carried full sail in a brisk wind that had an edge of chill about it. The declining sun left a bloodbath of colour over the Atlantic. Against it the line of black rocks off the southeast shore of Eileach-an-Naoimh, largest of the chain of four islands, lay sharply etched. We slipped in behind the outriding rocks to the recommended anchorage in 4 fathoms. The tide was full and a long, muscular swell rolled directly in from the south. *Hebe* rode it like a rollercoaster but the movement was uneasy and we were uncomfortably aware of the rocks just astern. At last light we moved to calm water amongst the Bold Islets and spent a quiet night. At low water we awoke to find *Hebe* resting serenely in a shallow pool completely surrounded by rocks. 'Bully for bilge keelers,' muttered Philip, my latest sailing companion, not entirely impressed by my choice of anchorage. Even if a strong wind had sprung up we would have been snug enough, but it is not an ideal place for a small boat. One is even more attentive about the slighest hint of change in wind, sky or sea. These are aptly named the Isles of the Sea, gaunt, abandoned and more of the sea than the land. Apart from the light beacon, a bright swatch of whitewash on the southern tip, there is no sign of modern life but plenty dating back to the time of Columba. By all accounts, the island is the long-lost Hinba of Adamnan's Life of St. Columba, the retreat used by Columba during his ministry on Iona. The number and extent of the ruins show that it was once an important religious centre. The Christian community on Eileach-an-Naoimh is supposed to have been founded by St. Brendan in AD 542, some twenty-one years before St. Columba arrived on Iona. The island is a high narrow spine of rock rising from the sea like some petrified wave. It is about 1 mile long by a ¼ of a mile wide. Inland, it is curiously rich in undergrowth with small glens and grassy hollows. The remains of the early settlement lie near the eastern edge in the centre of the island. There is a roofless chapel and beyond it a half-buried cavity where grain was once dried. Another underground chamber served as a cell for penitents seeking greater austerity. Between the main site and the eastern shore are two beehive cells. High on the ridge of the island with a stupendous view across the sea lies a grave marked by a stone bearing an incised cross. This is said to belong to Aethne, Columba's mother.

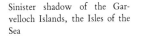

Sinister shadow of the Garvelloch Islands, the Isles of the Sea

As we explored the island, the first hint of mare's tails appeared in the sky. The forecast warned of increasing winds, so immediately *Hebe* rose well clear from her pool among the rocks we set sail and headed northwards to Mull. Our concern seemed a bit overdone when we saw a flotilla of canoeists heading cheerfully towards the island just as we were leaving.

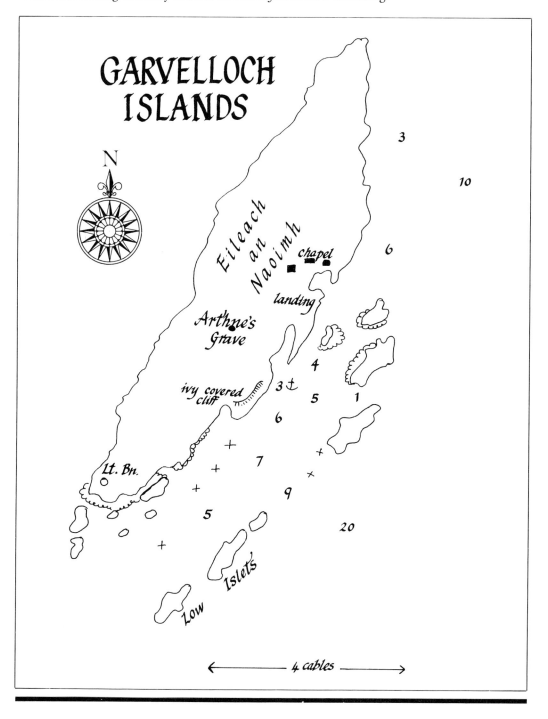

GARVELLOCH ISLANDS

N

Eileach an Naoimh

chapel

landing

Arthne's Grave

ivy covered cliff

Lt. Bn.

Low Islets

← —— 4 cables —— →

CORRY-VRECKAN

Map ref. 7E7
No facilities

The opening muster of the Royal Highland Yacht Club was to be a sort of mass tresspass through the Gulf of Corryvreckan. There were over 30 sailing boats and among them *Hebe* was by more than a foot the smallest. Elegant ketches, trim sloops and powerful launches (the safety boats) swilled around in the Dorus Mor awaiting the Commodore and his starting pennant. It was a fine morning; a light wind, warm sunshine sparkling off the sea and the gentle lap of gin and tonic over small shoals of ice. One vessel succeeded in stranding on the 2 ft.-rock just off Correagar with a thump that could be heard a quarter of a mile away. Fortunately it was a calm day and we were waiting for the westbound flood. The vessel was not holed and more damage was done to the skipper's pride than to the boat; he had sailed too close to Correagar with the Crinan Hotel hidden behind Craignish Point, a position that had put him within a wave length of the submerged rock.

Directly to the west lay the Gulf, the most notorious stretch of water off the west coast where the tide reaches 8 knots or more. When a westerly gale hits the spring flood there is a boiling of water that can be heard in

Haddock

N

Sca

7

19

deep c

GULF OF CO

20

Eilean Mor

20

12

Eilean Beg

7

Buige Rk.

3

Bagh Gleann nam Muc

Aird Bhreacain

6

4

3

Crinan. To the south lies Jura and to the north Scarba, both shores being iron-bound with rocks.

Even that day, with calm weather and a slack tide, there was an eerie atmosphere about the Gulf. The water had an unnaturally flat and brooding look, dotted with odd indents and whorls that sucked at the surface. Early writers described the passage alarmingly. 'The sea begins to boil and ferment with the tide of flood and resembles the boiling of a pot; and then increases gradually until it appears in many whirlpools, which form themselves in sort of pyramids and immediately after spout up as high as the mast of a little vessel, and at the same time make a loud report,' wrote Martin Martin. John MacCulloch declared: 'Corryvreckan is an enormous whirlpool which swallows up all ships that come within a mile of it. Impossible to be engaged in this place without anxiety. With every precaution, danger is always impending. The error of a few minutes might have been the price of as many lives' etc. The Clyde Cruising Club warns of dangerous overfalls and advises against attempting a passage with the flood in even moderate west winds.

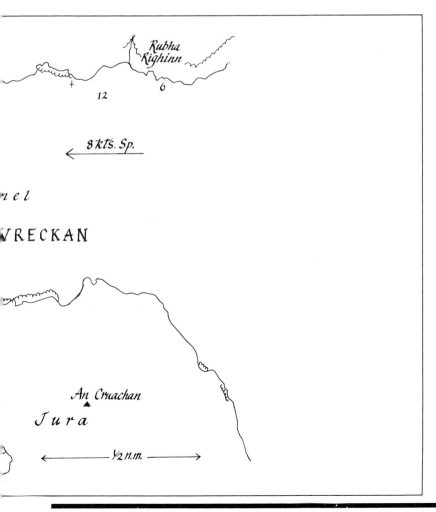

The spring muster was not haunted by any such banshees or Raillach (the old hag of a stormy sea). In the firm grip of the flood and with the motor roaring strongly to keep control and hold a course towards the Jura shore, *Hebe* hurtled through the Gulf sideways at about 7 knots. The muster instructions said that while the whole of the strait was clean and deep, a dangerous overfall lay about 2 cables off the south-west corner of Scarba that must be avoided at all times. Yachts *must* keep well south of the centre line but a strong tidal stream would be setting up the north-east side of Jura into Corryvreckan, propelling yachts towards the dangerous side. One stately sloop not fitted with an engine drifted straight into the vortex of the whirlpool and stuck there like the needle of a gramophone record. Fortunately there was no danger because of the gentle conditions and one of the power boats bustled in and towed him clear of the embryo maelstrom.

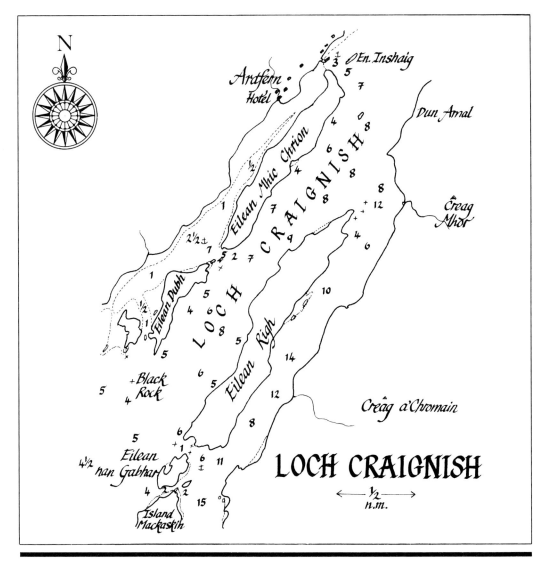

LOCH CRAIGNISH

Martin writes of an English ship being abandoned under all sail by her crew after she was caught up in the tide-race and went through unmanned to arrive on the shore of Knapdale undamaged. There are other legends, one of which explains how the Gulf got its name. Prince Bhreacan of Denmark fell in love with a maiden from Jura. Her father, who had no desire for a foreign sea-rover as son-in-law, refused his consent unless the prince undertook to spend three nights at anchor in the Gulf. The prince agreed to a condition that he would anchor his galley with three cables, the first of wool, the second of hemp and the third of the hair of maidens who had been true to their lovers. Alas for Bhreacan, all three cables parted and he was drowned.

Hebe quitted the Gulf like a cork from a champagne bottle, joining the rest of the fleet in a more sedate cruise down the west coast of Jura to Loch Tarbert and a barbecue on the beach. A fine day's sail.

ARDINAMIR

Map ref. 7F6
Water (at farm),
shop at Cullipool, 2m

From her parlour window Irene MacLachlan watches the entrance of Ardinamir anchorage with a keen and amused interest. The shoal that vessels must weave their way through, following the leading marks that she keeps fresh with white enamel paint, is hidden from view but she can tell from the moving mastheads showing above the arm of Ardinamir Bay whether a yacht is heading for problems. The smooth, round-topped reef has given her years of entertainment. To the luckless mariners whose

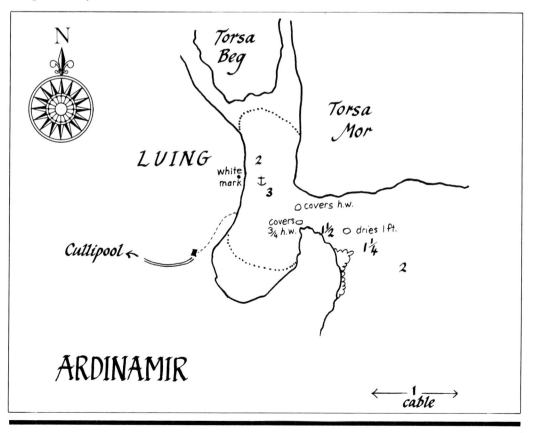

boats slide aground she advises: 'No use puffing and heaving and carrying on, you'll be there till the next tide'. Some seasons as many as four yachts in one day have grounded at the entrance. She has seen every kind of craft in this snug bay and bellowed at them to keep clear of the shallows at the southern end. Irene (who has been made an honorary life-member of the Clyde Cruising Club) has a voice that carries comfortably from Luing to Torsa Mor and a meticulously-kept log that records almost every craft that has arrived there since the days of the war. She remembers with affection the fine pre-plastic yachts with blocks that clattered and cotton sails that cracked to a tack and blended more suitably into the West Highland scenery. It is a very quiet life relieved by the arrival of long summer days that bring the crews of 400 yachts to her door. The world comes here, she says. Then there is that splendid local institution, the *Oban Times,* which she combs for literals. 'See this,' she guffaws, handing over the paper. It is the obituary of a local gardener 'who enjoyed most his sweet pees which he distributed generously amongst his friends'. Imagine printing that about the poor man.

Ardinamir Bay, Shuna Sound

To avoid an uncomplimentary note in Irene's log or a chilling blast from the headland, approach the anchorage on a course south of west, keeping 1½ cables from the south shore. When the white mark on the southern entrance bears 250° compass, head for it and avoid a reef extending from the southern headland. This course should also clear a rock in the middle of the channel. Stay close to the southern shore, avoiding another rock to port as the bay opens out, and a course of about 300° compass should lead to a white mark on rocks off the western shore. A second rock should slip by to starboard although both the last-mentioned rocks cover at high water. Anchor off the white mark in 2 fathoms.

Over the hill is an excellent restaurant with a fine view of Scarba Sound.

We ran into Easdale to escape a gale that was howling in from the direction of the Garvellochs and building up a steep unpleasant sea. The twin beacons marking the deep water of a channel prone to silt could be picked out easily and *Hebe* headed into Easdale Sound, leaving the black beacon to starboard and entering calmer waters. We entered a narrow, slate-surrounded gut leading off the south shore of the sound opposite the derelict pier and slipped into the quiet shelter of the harbour on Easdale Island - the perfect bolt-hole for a shallow-draft cruiser.

The remnants of the slate industry give Easdale and the island opposite a grey, neglected look which tourism and the search for second homes is slowly erasing. Small cottages, once the homes of quarry workers, are now being renovated and with a colourful lick of paint turned into miniature palaces. C. John Taylor's emporium is one of the most outrageous examples of how to cater for tourists, offering everything from a length of plaid to a portrait in oils of the Last Supper.

EASDALE

Map ref. 7E6
Seil Island: water, hotel, shop, PO

Easdale village

But slate was once the over-riding industry here, dating back to 1748 when commercial quarrying began, and towards the end of the eighteenth century five million slates a year were being produced.

The richest quarry was on Eilean-an-Beithich, an island of little more than two acres in Easdale Sound from which nine million slates were quarried each year until a high tide driven by a sou'westerly gale flooded the mine which by 1881 was 250 ft. below sea level. In those days the channel was busy with steamers, sloops and schooners, lining up to take away cargoes of slate. Once, the slate ships were the biggest source of revenue for the Crinan Canal. Now the place seems lifeless. A few small motorcraft are moored in the harbour but there are no big boats, and there is a strong risk that the sound will slowly silt up completely.

Telford's 'bridge over the Atlantic' near Puilladobhrain anchorage

Hebe was making a slicing north-easterly tack well clear of a coastline that had fractured into a maze of islets, skerries and submerged rocks over which low water was quietly licking. It was an ideal time to enter Puilladobhrain, one of the most acclaimed anchorages in the west; excellent shelter, good holding ground when the forecast was for strong north-westerly winds and a fine pub over the hill, the door of which would at that very moment be opening for custom.

PUILLA-DOBHRAIN

Map ref. 4A3
Clachan Bridge: hotel,

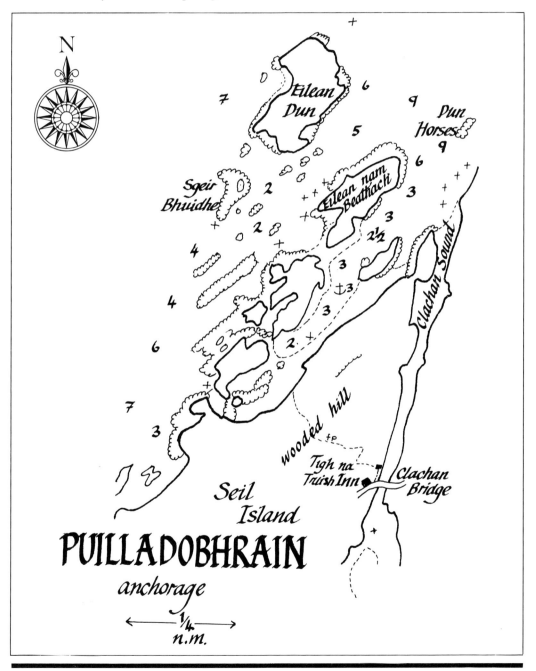

N

Eilean Dun

Dun Horses

Sgeir Bhuidhe

Eilean nam Beathach

Clachan Sound

wooded hill

Tigh na Truish Inn

Clachan Bridge

Seil Island

PUILLADOBHRAIN

anchorage

¼ n.m.

Dave observed that the chart around Eilean Dun had more crosses on it than the average graveyard, so we stood well off and rounded the north shore of the island until we were reaching across 9 fathoms of calm water to the tip of Eilean nam Beithach. The rocks of the Dun Horses were clear to see and *Hebe* made a stately entrance, anchoring in three fathoms in the middle of this 'Pool of the Otter'. Our navigation notes describe white cairns on the islands giving a leading line and a white cross west of the entrance marking a rock.

The bad rock at the southern end of the pool was more emphatically marked, the first time I sailed in here, by a fishing boat that had stranded upon it. Now those remains had drifted off into the reef to the west.

There were only a couple of other boats sharing the pool with us. One was a handsome wooden cutter with a high coach roof and a crew of three elderly folk who pottered about their duties to the sound of music which drifted from the cabin. From the mainland shore a footpath climbs the hillside and drops down to the road at the Tigh na Truish Hotel, known locally as 'the house of the trousers'. The story goes that in the days when wearing Highland dress was forbidden the islanders of Seil would hand in their illegal kilts in exchange for a pair of breeks in which they could travel to town.

The handsome bridge near the hotel spans Clachan Sound between Seil and the mainland and was completed in 1793 from plans by Thomas Telford. It is a high arch of local grey slate that once allowed substantial vessels to pass beneath it. Silting has badly affected the narrow channel, the north end of which dries out at low water. Telford's 'Bridge over the Atlantic' is a natural rockery for a bright collection of alpine plants that grow, beyond an arm's length, in the crevices of the parapet.

Puilladobhrain entrance

Perhaps we left Easdale too soon. The wind had veered into the north-west and *Hebe* now lay on her ear with a line of rolls in the main and working jib pulling hard. The bows chopped the Firth of Lorne like a blunt axe.

She was already showing her propensity for weather helm and I longed for a couple of feet extra on the water line. Still, she was gamely making about 3 knots into a Force 5 that was whipping off the tide. Weather helm can be a curse in a bilge keeler and to shorten sail further would only reduce her punching power. I remembered the fully fledged gale we had bludgeoned our way through once when the helmsman gradually increased the helm to weather until the tiller was so hard over he was sitting with his back pressed hard against it. And still her head pressed towards the eye of the wind. He took hold of the tiller and pushed a little harder. Suddenly the woodwork tore itself free of the jaws. Such a squint of surprise as he was left holding a lifeless club I had not seen since the vicar picked up an exploding fork.

Each bang of the bows produced its own echo below as the contents of the cabin readjusted themselves. A trickle of red on the cabin sole showed that the Bull's Blood had leaked, a small tide of soup was spreading across the coast of Mull (on the chart) and things were becoming sordid.

'Spelve,' said Dave, as a wave slapped his cheek like a challenge. I was happy to agree and sorted out a course. The entrance lay a couple of miles ahead, a cleavage in the east coast of Mull. To the south the coast curves round in a range of stupendous cliffs that are a bulwark against the Atlantic; wild and exposed. As we closed the coast we felt some shelter but the hills shifted the wind about oddly. The entrance was draining and we wondered whether the engine would beat the departing 3-knot tide.

LOCH SPELVE

Map ref. 7E5
No facilities; entrance may be difficult in strong south-westerlies

Hebe at anchor, Loch Spelve

Perhaps we miscalculated because by the time we picked out and headed for the dark shoulder on the north shore, the water felt slack and in the narrow entrance channel there were fronds of kelp almost reaching the surface. The 2 fathoms near the confusion of white markers seemed optimistic if anything, but since *Hebe* will slide through a little more than half a fathom we felt secure.

Soon the anvil-shaped loch opened out, a lonely and imposing place. A swift beat brought us to Eilean Amolaig but the anchorage there was occupied by a seafarm. *Hebe* hardened up towards a cluster of boats anchored near the beach where the Lussa River pours into the loch. This proved snug enough, particularly as the wind backed into the south-west leaving us protected by a high birch-covered bluff on shore.

It took two hours next morning to beat down to the far end of the loch to examine the anchorage there which seemed to be open to a wind tunnel in the westerlies. The wind comes tumbling up Loch Buie and is funnelled by the mountains directly into Spelve where it may arrive in very bad temper. Certainly on the run eastwards, we were clear of the loch and far out into the Firth of Lorne within half an hour. Remember, follow the wind for a peaceful life.

Common Tern. Nests in colonies, sometimes with other terns and gulls on shingle and saltings; assembles in flocks in autumn

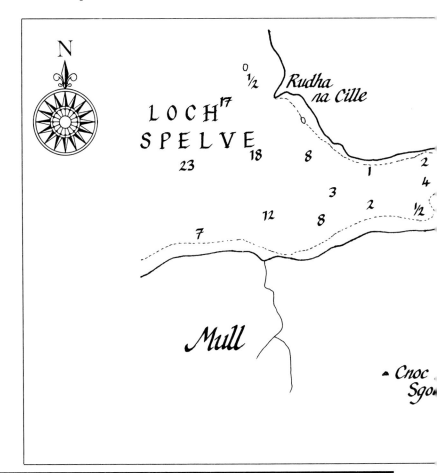

Entrance to Loch Spelve from Mull

Mull

4
2 8 2
½
2 11 3 *Rudha na Faoilinn*
1 4
tha nan ailthean 10
4
2
7
3

LOCH
SPELVE
← ½ →
n.m.

THE LYNE OF LORNE

Map ref. 8A6
Port Ramsay: water (by pier)
Port Appin: water, hotel, shop, PO

There are some excellent small anchorages where there is little chance of being disturbed by the ceaseless slap of other people's halyards or the bedlam of the fleshpots. Port Ramsay on the northern end of Lismore has an intricate entrance through a litter of rocks and islets and *Hebe* spent a quiet night tucked behind Eilean Nain Meahn. The warm weather returned next day as the skies cleared and the broad waters of the loch lay shimmering. Lismore is a long and beautiful island, fertile and green, taking its name from the Gaelic equivalent of 'Great Garden'. It is surrounded by superb landscapes and seascapes. It became Christian in the sixth century when St. Moluag, a contemporary of St. Columba, lived there. In the thirteenth century the diocese of Argyll had its cathedral on the island after the Scottish episcopate was established in obedience to Rome. Few traces of this once important building remain. Lismore was the birthplace of John Stuart McCaig whose 'Folly' de grandeur overlooks the town of Oban; a colossus of a folly started to give work to unemployed masons and finished as an ego trip for the Oban art critic, philosophical essayist and banker. Further east from the tip of Lismore is Port Appin where we stopped temporarily to take on stores and water. There is a good grocery here together with Post Office and telephone.

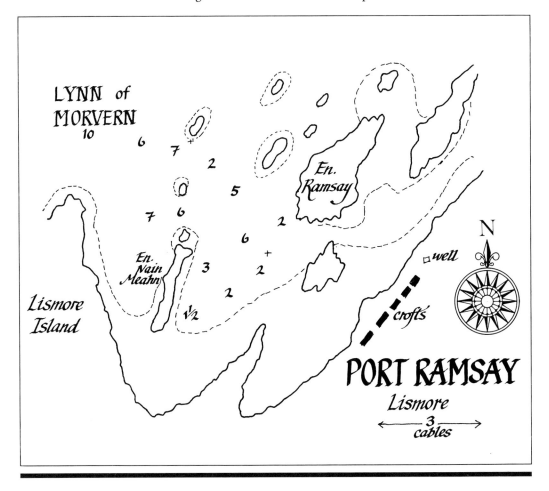

LYNN of MORVERN

En. Ramsay

Lismore Island

En. Nain Meahn

N

well

crofts

PORT RAMSAY
Lismore
3 cables

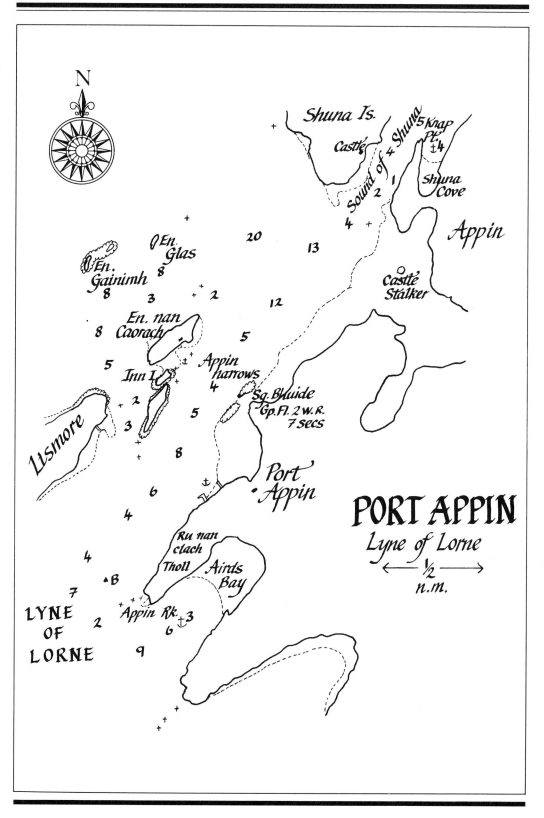

N

Shuna Is.

Castle

Sound of Shuna

5 Knap Pt.
±4

Shuna Cove

Appin

2

4

1

20

13

En. Glas

En. Gainimh
8

8

3

2

12

Castle Stalker

En. nan Caorach

8

5

Appin narrows

Inn I.

5

2

4

Sg. Bhuide
Gp. Fl. 2 w. R.
7 secs

3

5

Lismore

8

Port Appin

6

4

PORT APPIN

Lyne of Lorne

← ½ →
n.m.

Ru nan clach

Tholl

Airds Bay

4

B

7

Appin Rk.

2

6

±3

LYNE
OF
LORNE

9

Here is the ancient land of the Stewarts of Appin who round about 1500 built Castle Stalker, the fine-looking fortress on an island in Loch Laich. The building stood as a hunting lodge used by James IV and eventually fell into ruins. It has since been restored and now stands on its loch-bound knoll looking much as it did in the sixteenth century. We later regretted passing the good anchorage in the lee of Sheep Island near the Appin narrows and instead ghosted around Shuna Island - we were unsure of the depth in the Sound of Shuna - and turned into Shuna Cove, a sheltered bay surrounded by wooded shore. Unfortunately the aroma drifting from a poultry enterprise at the southern end takes the edge off this anchorage. We walked that evening along a disused railway where trees form a tunnel down which hundreds of bats swoop and flock at dusk.

Castle Stalker

LOCH CORRIE

Map ref. 8A6
No facilities

It is easy to pick out Loch Corrie across Loch Linnhe. The large indent in the Morvern shore appeared once we had cleared the Sound of Shuna (the tide was high this time) and jibed gently onto a north-westerly course with the sails pulling well and *Hebe* set on a long fetch for the loch mouth. The sailing instructions warn of violent squalls in strong winds and that was understandable since the shores of the loch rise into long high mountain ridges. Far from brewing squalls, the high land robbed us of wind and our gentle entry into that imposing loch was watched by a pair of eagles circling above Sgurr a Bhuic. The anchor sank into deep, peaty water close to the south shore and a little distance from a cottage near two lines of birch trees. The hills around the loch were fine for a leg-stretch and we returned tired and ready for the lamb chops and fresh veg. we had bought earlier. We had been sailing for some days and my daughters were growing anxious about the possibility of scurvy and were examining their tongues for grey tendrils. It was a fine night with a full moon turning the still waters of the loch to silver. The girls were snug asleep, *Hebe* stirred quietly at anchor as the outgoing tide slipped by; the

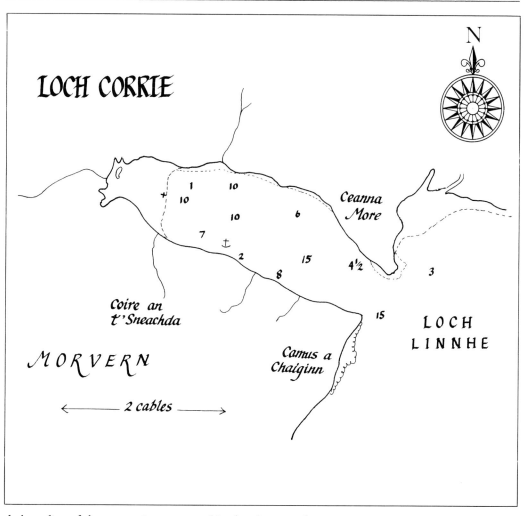

dark outline of the mountains was traced in the glimmer of stars. Frances handed up a glass of glüwein made with a base of warmed Bull's Blood. Perfick, as Pop Larkin would say, perfick.

We were up early next morning to catch the ebb. The wind had got up and was considerably blowing directly out of the mouth of the loch. We put up the sails, lifted the anchor and *Hebe* gently turned to point her bow eastwards. As we left the loch and the shelter of the shore the wind, distorted by the hills, went through 90 degrees. As we turned south our run became a fine beat down the Morvern shore with tack following tack until the tide turned and we anchored off the four-square ruin of Gruagaich Castle in one of the most deserted parts of Morvern.

The castle stands ideally positioned on a hill overlooking the sea. Little is known about its history but it was probably built in the fifteenth century as a stronghold of the Macleans of Kingairloch. The story goes that a pirate named Runie once used the fortress as a base for raids on the surrounding countryside. On one of these plundering missions into Appin on the opposite shore of Loch Linnhe he camped on the ground where Appin

House now stands. A few braver local souls crept up on the camp while the pirates were feasting and dislodged a large boulder on the hill above. It crashed down on the camp, killing Runie and two of his sons and scattering the rest. Beyond the castle lies the deserted valley of Glensanda, with its ruined crofts and broad sweep of fertile but neglected land.

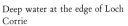

Caisteal Na Gruagaich, Morvern

Deep water at the edge of Loch Corrie

The entrance to the Sound of Mull from the south offers a choice of anchorages; fleshpots to the left, solitude to the right. After tacking down
the coast of Morvern and lingering off Gruagaich Castle we had missed
the tide up the sound and decided to spend the night in the perfect secluded anchorage behind Rudha an Ridire. The hook bit into sand in the
shelter of a small cluster of islands close to a shore that rises steeply and
sweeps round in a high cliff down which a waterfall tumbles. In spate
these falls are quite spectacular and are known as the Morvern Witches.
At the highest point of the cliff there is a large flat stone known as the
Rock of Corpses. The story goes that prisoners of the Chiefs of Ardtornish who were condemned to death were hurled over the cliffs from here.

The wreck of a puffer can be seen protruding from the water of one of
the islands which lies on another wreck which is said to be close to a third
wreck of an English warship, HMS *Dartmouth,* sent to harry the Scots,
which foundered there.

SOUND OF MULL

Map ref. 7E4
Craignure: water,
shop, PO

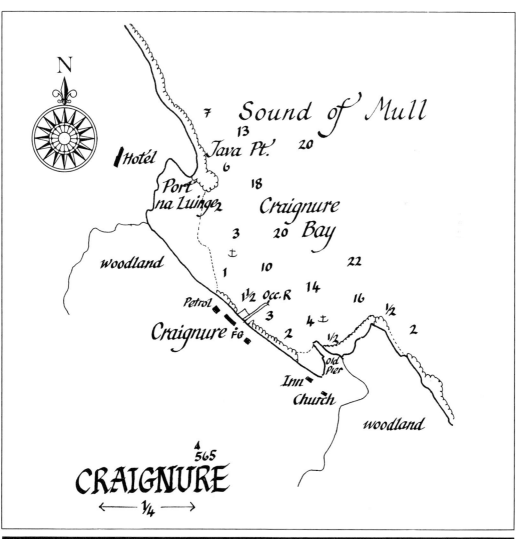

Next morning we motored into the wind across the Sound of
Craignure and tied up alongside the *Eldesa,* the last working 'puffer' on
the west coast. Her skipper, Mr. Hugh Carmichael, who was born on
Lismore, is a man with the quiet humour and the true West Highland
dignity of Para Handy himself. The *Eldesa* for many years ran loads of logs
felled in the Forestry Commission plantation on Mull from Craignure to
Corpach at the head of Loch Linnhe. The closure of the pulp mill there
meant an end to the log run. The tendrils of recession reach even this quiet
place. The other event in recent history, which had shades of 'Whisky
Galore' about it, was when a large cache of cannabis hidden or dumped in
the Sound of Mull drifted ashore and mingled with the kelp and sea
tangle. Gentlemen from Her Majesty's Customs and Excise suddenly appeared on the foreshore like energetic beach-combers. The place where a
lot of the stuff came ashore was called, prophetically as it proved, Grass
Point. There were reports of hens, wont to peck and scratch about the
beach, laying painfully large eggs and behaving strangely. 'I could swear
one of my hens thought he was a policeman, just by the swagger that
came on him. He was hallucinating, I suppose, poor thing,' one crofter
told me.

There is fair holding ground in Craignure Bay just north of the pier
where the ferry from Oban is a regular caller. Craignure has a well-
stocked store, Post Office, fuel supplies and water. Shallow-draught
vessels may find it easier to tuck behind the old pier which is close to the
Craignure Inn.

Hebe alongside *Eldsea* at Craignure pier, Isle of Mull

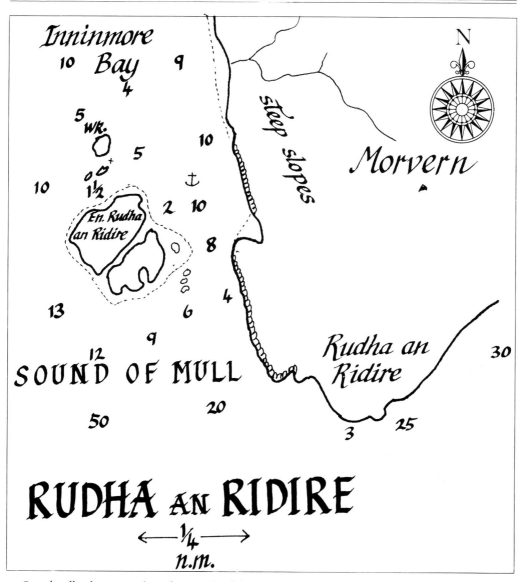

Inninmore Bay

10 9

4

5 wk.

5

10

10

⚓

En. Rudha an Ridire

1½

2 10

8

13

6

4

9

12

SOUND OF MULL

20

50

steep slopes

Morvern

N

Rudha an Ridire

30

3 25

RUDHA AN RIDIRE

←— ¼ —→

n.m.

On a headland commanding the mouth of the Sound and every inch of what a fortress should be stands Castle Duart, home of the Chiefs of the Macleans of Duart. Built in the thirteenth century, the castle has sixteenth and seventeenth century additions. It was occupied by the Macleans until the seventeenth century when the Marquess of Argyll dominated the Maclean family. The Macleans lost the lands after the clan had held out for James II at Cairnburg Mor fortress in the Treshnish Islands until 1691. The castle was then garrisoned by the government until the end of the 18th century. Sir Fitzroy Maclean, 10th baronet and 26th Chief of Duart, bought the building back and lifted it from decay by the time of his death in 1936. Wounded in the Crimean campaign - he charged with the Light Brigade - and given only a few days to live, the doughty chief lived on to be more than 100 years old.

One well-known skeleton in the Maclean of Duart cupboard relates to the chief who married a sister of the Earl of Argyll and fell out with her seriously enough for him to maroon her, in 1530, on Lady Rock off the south end of Lismore. This harsh treatment led to a clan feud which ended in Maclean's slaughter. On the opposite shore of Duart Bay lies Torosay Castle, a handsome mid-Victorian example of Scottish baronial style. It was completed in 1858 by David Bryce, a leading architect of that formidable school. It has a superb terraced garden laid out by Sir Robert Lorimer, the Capability Brown of the Edwardian era. There are interesting family records in both castles.

'Puffer' aground, Sound of Mull

LOCH ALINE

Map ref. 6E4
Water (at jetty), shops, PO

The tide pours swiftly in and out of Loch Aline and it is a hard battle sailing in if the contents of the loch are being decanted at the time. We waited in Ardtornish Bay, 1 mile east of the entrance to the loch, and explored the remains of Ardtornish Castle, one-time stronghold and seat of government of the great Lords of the Isles, now a mouldering ruin.

We sailed *Hebe* on the first of the flood into Loch Aline. The village on the north bank has shops and petrol and a doctor who lives at the top of the hill. A quarry near the town tends to be noisy. There is no good anchorage on the village side of the loch because of the tides, the ferry to Fishnish and the lack of a good place to tie up. The most sheltered spot we found was behind Kyle Point in a lovely, wooded bay. It was a pleasant walk from here to Kinlochaline Castle at the head of the loch. The building is a fifteenth century tower house, reputedly the traditional home of the Clan MacInnes, hereditary bowmen to the Clan MacKinnon. It is said to have been built by Lady Dhubh Chal (Black Veil) and paid for in butter of a volume equal to that of the castle. One local name for the building is Caisteal an Ime, or Butter Castle. Its 7ft.-thick walls were breached by Cromwell's army. Above the door are openings for pouring burning oil and hot lead onto the heads of besiegers. The building was restored in 1890 and it is possible occasionally to look round the interior.

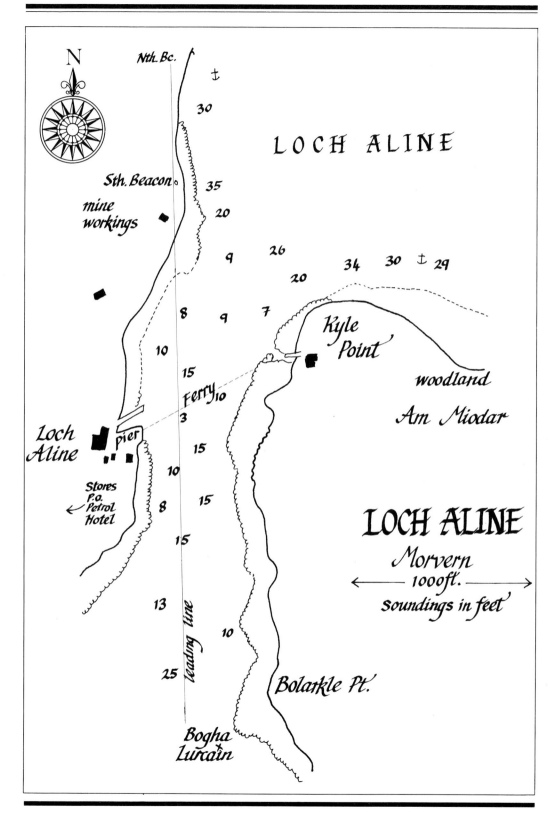

N

Nth. Bc.

LOCH ALINE

30

Sth. Beacon   35
mine   20
workings
                    26
              9   34   30   ⚓ 29
                   20
        8   9   7
                         Kyle
    10   Point
                                woodland
    15
        Ferry 10   Am Miodar
Loch   3
Aline pier
        15
Stores 10
P.O.
← Petrol   15
Hotel   8

        15   LOCH ALINE
                        Morvern
    13   ←—— 1000ft. ——→
                    soundings in feet
        10

    25

Bogha   Bolarkle Pt.
Lurcain

SALEN

Map ref. 7D4
Water (at pier), hotel,
shop, PO; avoid in
easterlies

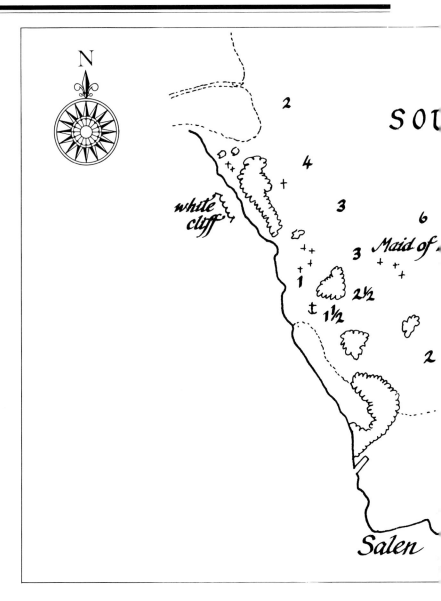

The wind died, the engine broke down and *Hebe* lay drifting at slack water off Salen. We used the dinghy oars rigged onto the cockpit edge to propel her laboriously into Salen. We approached the derelict-looking pier, having drifted well clear of the Bo Rock and its outlying obstacles, when the breeze piped up again from the land. It was just enough to send *Hebe* at a directable drift to the west end of the bay leaving the red buoy marking the Antelope Rock to port and heading for the white patch of quartz on a cliff above the road. We ghosted close to the rocks before turning behind them and anchoring in the sheltered water near two yachts lying to permanent moorings. It was a snug place to cook a meal and then wander down the road to the Salen Hotel. One of the yachts belonged to the doctor at Salen who sailed in it from America.

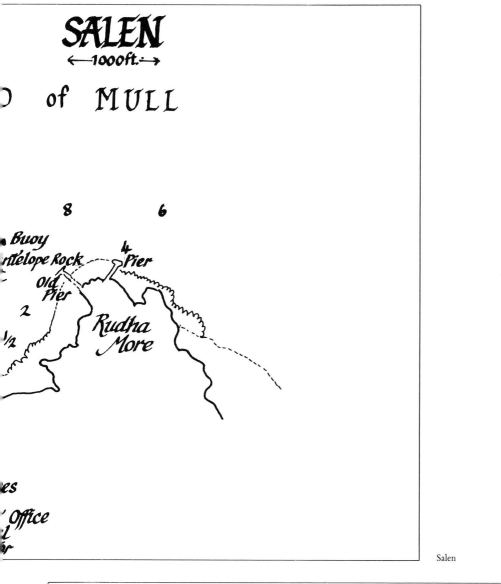

SALEN
←1000ft.→

of MULL

8   6

Buoy
ntelope Rock   4 Pier
    Old
    Pier
  2
½
        Rudha
        More

es
Office

Salen

TOBERMORY

Map ref. 6D3
All facilties available

We sailed up the northern leg of the Sound of Mull with the genoa boomed out, the main goose-winged and a stiff breeze dead astern. A flock of other yachts all riding the same tide cruised past, bright spinnakers billowing with a kind of aldermanic roundness. Calve Island, which shelters Tobermory, slipped by to port and the harbour front opened up. The town is a gem. Solid-looking but delightfully proportioned buildings form a curving and colourful line along the sea front. The bay is well sheltered by wooded hills and has a number of anchorages to match any direction of the wind.

On that day it was fairly snorting in, raising goose pimples among the small clutch of bathers on the sandy beach and rattling the halyards of about 50 yachts anchored off the town. I usually took the helm entering harbour (for no better reason than that the owner's name looks better on the insurance claim), but Trevor's knuckles were a white row where he gripped the tiller and there was a stubborn cut to his chin. The whisker pole was stowed and we were broad-reaching at high speed by *Hebe* standards for the shore across the bows of the anchored armada. The plan was to slip around the edge of the fleet and reach back to a point opposite the

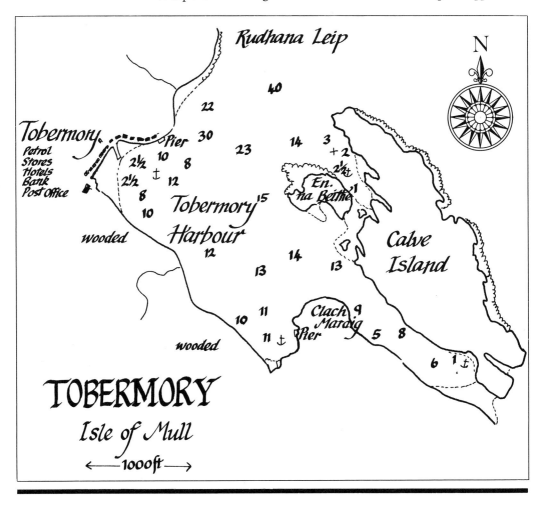

Mishnish pub. The plan went well at first. 'Over there?' Trevor pointed to a clear patch beyond a small cruiser, smaller even than *Hebe*, made of dyspeptic mint-green plastic. 'Fine,' I said, clearing the anchor and yanking up a fathom or so of chain. *Hebe* reached the appointed spot, put her head into the wind and down went the hook into the Tobermory mud. Trevor was reaching for a celebratory bottle of Bull's Blood when we became aware that the mint-green cruiser was hoving rapidly towards us, or more accurately we towards it. The jib sheet had snarled, the anchor had clearly bitten about as hard as a toothless hamster and *Hebe* was making one of her usual swoops to l'ward before sailing on.

'Fend off!' I howled, wildly letting out lengths of chain. There was a sickening crash and we could hear the sound of crockery breaking, cutlery spilling out of drawers and weighty objects leaving their accustomed resting places. The cruiser had its curtains drawn but seemed undamaged. *Hebe* drew away to a point where we could sort out the mess, put the anchor down again and drift gently back on the wind to allow it to bite. Back we went with increasing speed but with none of the firm, terrier tug and slight shaking of the bows to indicate a successfully buried anchor. I let out more chain but the stern-first progress continued. 'You can't guess what's about to happen,' said Trevor, reaching for a clutch of fenders. He augmented them with his feet, which are uncommonly large, to ease the collision with the small cruiser to which *Hebe* seemed to be magnetically attracted. The crash was rather less this time but still enough to rock the vessel and produce a few tinkling sounds from below.

At that moment the curtains were wrenched apart. A head appeared wearing a hat clearly intended for a high admiral of the Pomeranian Navy to judge from the festoons of gold wire embroidering its peak. Looking down on him we could see that apart from the hat the man was stark naked and in a state of angry excitement. He had obviously ignored the

Tobermory Bay crowded with yachts after the Tobermory race

first sudden barrage of cups, saucers and other nautical moveables but the second assualt from the teaspoons had been too much. Because Trevor's feet were the first things he saw when he pulled back the curtains his eyes were squinting, which added to his look of wrath. 'All this harbour, all the bloody harbour and you have to pick on us,' he bellowed at the feet. The curtains snapped shut. There was a heavy emphasis on the 'us'. We anchored successfully a discreet distance away.

The wind blew strongly during the rest of the day and the harbour quickly filled up, many boats sensibly seeking better shelter at the southern end near the derelict pier beyond Clach Maraig. Another fine corner to tuck into is the bay in the south-west of Calve Island. The barometer was falling sharply, the sky filled with ominous, tell-tale clouds and we opted to stay in Tobermory and by patient experiment decide whether the MacDonald Arms with its shelves groaning with every malt in creation outweighed the attractions of the Mishnish which has the talented attraction of Bobbie MacLeod's accordion. Both are warm, convivial places to be on a dreich day. One local, asked to express his preference between the two after he had clearly put in several years of conscientious comparison, put it: 'Inteed, if there iss any deeference at aal, they are poth the same, especially the Mishnish'.

I took bits of our broken-down engine, including the sparking plugs, to the garage where a motorist who was having his car filled up was talking to a yachtsman about his drive there from Basingstoke as if he were describing a voyage. 'Fine run all the way. Hint of rain but I left things as they were. Didn't touch the wiper once'. Odd how you can relish the minutiae of sailing but not the sterile boredom of driving a car.

The old pier at Tobermory

Inside the garage a solemn lad named Angus offered my plugs to a rather aged sand-blasting machine which left them rather more tarnished than they had been. 'She's no blasting,' he said, fiddling with the adjustments. Still the machine refused to work. The manager appeared and examined it. 'Perhaps if you whackled it,' Angus suggested to him. 'Whackle!' said the manager recoiling from a word that suggested such an unscientific form of coercion. 'I'll tell you, Angus, this garage operates on proper enchineering principles. I will get the instruction book'. Immediately he was gone, Angus gave the machine a mighty wallop with a spanner. A stream of grit trickled from the bottom but when he pressed the lever a scouring jet of sand blasted upwards. His solemn face broke into a triumphant grin. Back at the boat I inserted the plugs and gave the engine a kick. It worked perfectly. You can't whack a good whackle.

Ru Na Gal Light, Tobermory

LOCH SUNART

Map ref. 6E3

It is usually assumed that sailing from Tobermory means heading north around Ardnamurchan or round to the superb western edge of Mull. The seeker after quiet corners need voyage no further than the sheltered waters of Loch Sunart. The wind was still bellowing from the south-west, the skies were overcast and the glass lingering around bottom C when we left Tobermory Bay. With a well-reefed main and the smallest jib we set a course for the haughty rib of Maclean's Nose on Ardnamurchan, which was just visible.

Hebe held course with rain-drenched sails, gurgling purposefully along. The thickening weather wiped away Maclean's Nose and reduced the wash to a dim grey line. It was the west at its worst. Suddenly the buoy marking the New Rocks appeared to port. We were not blessed with a log but there was nothing else the forlorn-looking marker could have been, so we set a course slightly north of east which would clear both the Red Rocks and Big Stirk and soon Auliston Head appeared in the gloom. The south-west wind gave a few more derisory blasts before *Hebe* slid into the lee of the coast, still going at top speed towards a dead end in the angle of the coast.

Puffin. Fish-eater which
breeds in colonies in burrows on off-shore islets
and cliff tops

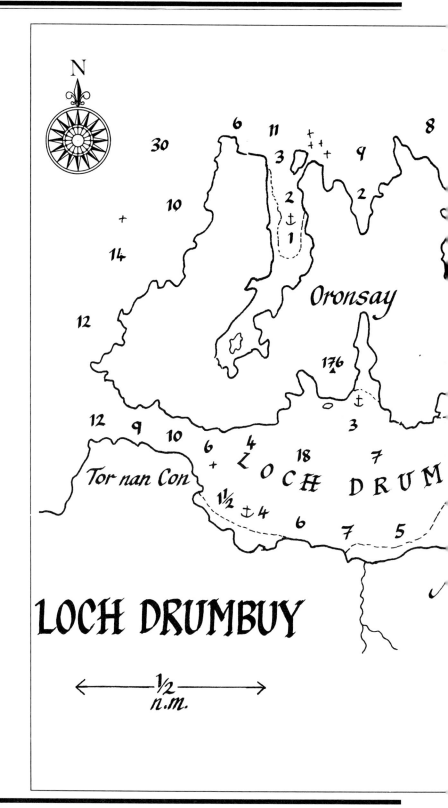

LOCH DRUMBUY

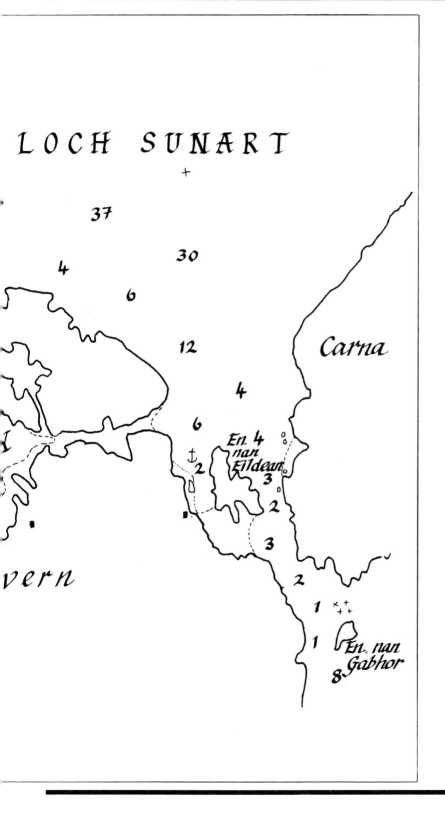

LOCH DRUMBUY

Map ref. 6D3
No facilities

The sailing instructions described Loch Drumbuy as a perfectly sheltered anchorage but the entrance is not perfectly apparent on such a day. 'It's there all right. I mean it can't be a Clyde Cruising Club wheeze, can it?' Trevor said. The dark rocks of the coast closed in forbiddingly. The shore was clear now, hard-shouldered and decorated with stretches of drenched moss. *Hebe* sailed into a narrow gap no more than half a cable wide between the Morvern shore and the island of Oronsay. The channel was deep but the instructions warned of a rock off the south point with 3 ft. over it. The narrows formed a key to a perfect anchorage, quite unspoilt and with no sign of civilisation about it. The usual anchorage is in the south-west corner but a large raft of jolly sailing folk, the jingle of bottles and the appearance on his flying bridge of a man in immaculate white ducks, encouraged us to slip behind a rock on the opposite side of the loch where we were protected from everything.

Trevor was below, tearing the entrails from a couple of mackerel, warming up a sponge pudding and bringing the Bull's Blood up to body temperature by putting the bottle into a pan of boiling water. The rain beat down on the flat surface of the loch, water hung like jewellery along the branches of trees and on the high hillside opposite a number of burns had burst into silvery torrents. A heron watching *Hebe* from the bank when a lump of entrails flew from the hatch and over the side, launched himself in lumbering, reptilian flight to the opposite shore. There was a waft of warmth from below, the rich whiff of grilled mackerel and the bite of wine brought almost to boiling point (it is virtually impossible to destroy the qualities of Bull's Blood). I was dry inside my oilskins, the circulation was returning with a sting to my face and the rain could not destroy the impression of a fine day's sail.

ORONSAY

Map ref. 6D3
No facilities

Oronsay suggests an island which in fact is connected to the mainland at low water. Such is the case with Loch Sunart's Oronsay (to be distinguished from the islet off Colonsay) which has a deep gut in its northern shore bedded with the most glutinous mud. An old gaff cutter drifted into Oronsay, a splendid pitch-black vessel that reeked of tar and tradition with limp tan sails. There was a rattle of hoops running down the mast and the clatter of blocks as the mainsail descended - a noise rarely heard today. From somewhere within the old girl's innards a paraffin engine wheezed into life and took her on a brief, stately tour of the gut. The skipper dropped a lead line over the side and sensed the sticky suck of the mud and shook his head. He was concerned that his anchor, an iron monster that squatted menacingly on the fore deck, might well sink irretrievably into the bed of glue and also that there might not be enough swinging room for his vessel. He left in search of space and clean sand.

The island once had a community living on it because it formed part of a drove trail south from Ardnamurchan. The derelict walls of a number of crofts remain. It is a totally remote and sheltered place, a bay full of duck and seal but with an entrance that requires care. The ground to the east is very foul. (For chart, see Loch Drumbuy above).

Ruined croft, Oronsay

Shortening sail off Oronsay

LOCH TEACHDAIS

Map ref. 6E3
No facilities

The weather forecast that evening could have been set to music by Wagner, Mussorgsky or any other musician given to heavy gloom and a powerful wind section. The loch was cold, grey and unpleasant. *Hebe* with shortened sail turned east when clear of the foul ground and followed the edge of Oronsay, turning down the narrow channel where Carna Island lies like a loose stopper in the mouth of Loch Teachdais. This western entrance is not advisable for deep-draught craft. Even *Hebe* felt her way gingerly through the channel which showed every sign of not having much water in it. The tide was just starting to flood into the loch so things would have been much easier if we had waited an hour or so. Past Eileann nan Gabhar where the water deepens and the wider channel from Loch Sunart flows in from the north-east, watery sunshine began to break through the clouds and powerful shafts of light revived the scenery. The difference was startling. Colour sprang back into the trees and countryside and danced on the water. The wind was still strong in the sky but Teachdais was well protected by steep, forested sides.

We anchored opposite Rahoy House, the manor of Rahoy estate which was bought by the Highlands and Islands Development Board. The estate can only be reached, by land, down several miles of spring-breaking track that should be strewn with the exhaust systems of luckless saloons. A large part of the land is given over to farming deer, in the same way that sheep are farmed, in the hope of finding an alternative economic use for barren Highland areas. There is a sprinkling of holiday homes here as well. Above Rahoy House and on a hilltop overlooking the entrance to the loch lie the remains of a fort. There are some fine walks here on both sides of the loch.

The next day sparkled into life in perfect high summer style with the weather forecast scrambling to catch up with reality. We had breakfast of fresh prawns washed down with a very fine bottle of Moselle - an unfaithful lapse, but Bull's Blood would have insulted the shellfish. As we prepared to set sail the wind swung obligingly into the south-east and we drifted up lovely Loch Teachdais with the young ebb, taking the channel east of Carna. Sgeir Liath at the southern end of the narrows was marked by a log perch and we followed the crooked course around the two obstructions in the channel until Loch Sunart opened out and we could jibe westwards. With the red sandstone towers of Glenborrodale Castle gliding by to starb'd *Hebe* picked up her skirts and made for the sea.

Rahoy House, Loch Teachdais

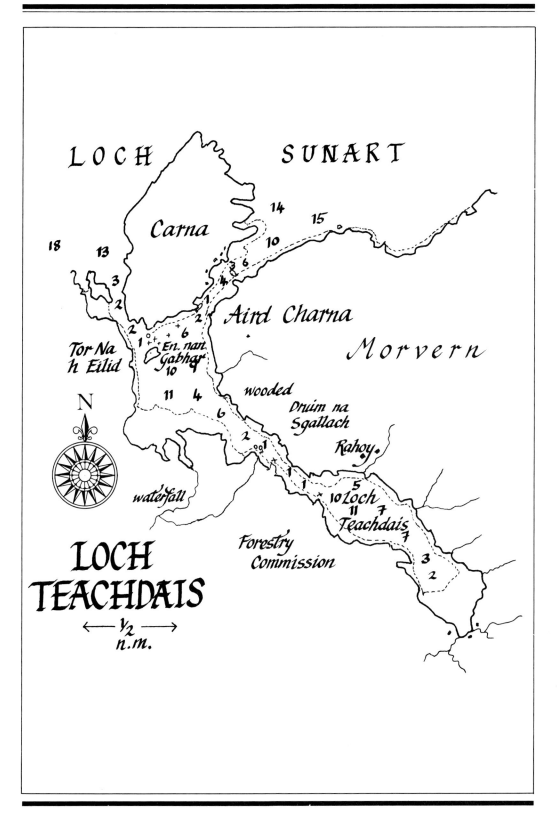

LOCH SUNART

Carna

18   13

3

2

2

Tor Na
h Eilid

1 o +   + 6
+ En. nan
Gabhar
10

N

11   4

6

waterfall

14

15

10

6
4

1

2

Aird Charna

Morvern

wooded

Druim na
Sgallach

Rahoy

2

1

1

1

5

10 Loch
11   Teachdais 7

Forestry
Commission

3

2

LOCH
TEACHDAIS
←— ½ —→
n.m.

COLL

Map ref. 6A3
Water (pump), hotel,
shops, PO; avoid in
a south-easterly

It had been deceiving to be in the shelter of Loch Sunart. Out past Ard-more Point where the big waves began, the shore of Mull shrank rapidly astern. The south-east wind was strong but the forecast said it would reduce in strength so we headed along 267° for Arinagour on Coll. The wind clearly had a tail which had escaped the Metman's calculations. By late afternoon it was blowing furiously directly into the Coll anchorage. *Hebe* passed between Bogha Mor and the scattering of inshore reefs and made for where we could see a bristle of masts tossing in the rollers. The tide was ebbing and the waves were breaking a couple of cables astern of us. A large German yacht ahead of us moved further out and re-anchored for fear that the keel might put in a sudden appearance through the cabin sole.

We put down a couple of anchors and had the third prepared and wat-ched the Germans sitting in the cockpit of their yacht whilst it roller-coasted the waves. There would have been no advantage to us in moving to the alternative anchorage at the eastern side of the reef. A couple of boats in there already were shifting about wildly. We were on a lee shore whether we liked it or not and would have to sit it out. The anchor warp ran from the bow at a shallow angle away to the distant hook. In the troughs it looked nearly parallel with the water - a sure sign that the depth was minimal. We pulled out towards the Germans, *Hebe's* engine barely able to make way against the wind and the surge of the sea. It then started to rain.

The old landing stage, Coll

right Loch Drumbuy from the distance
over Oronsay North, off Loch Sunart. Watch for the glutinous mud at the head of the anchorage

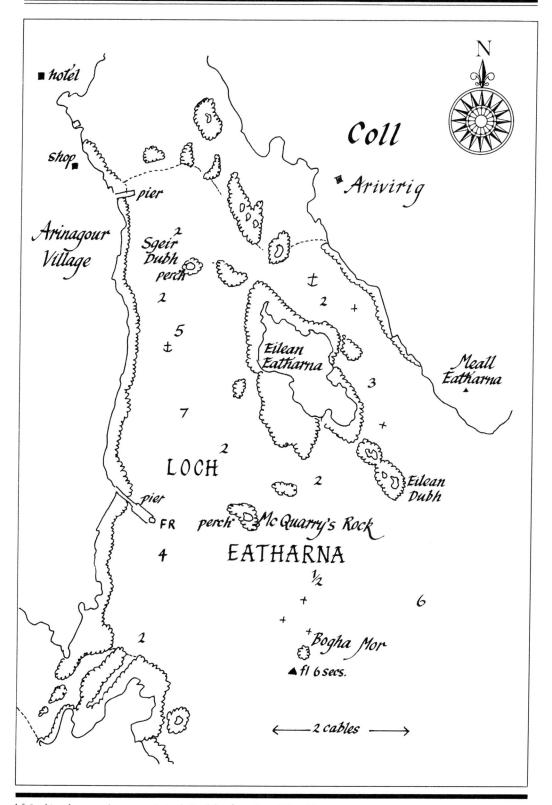

N

■ hotel

shop ■

pier

Arinagour
Village

Sgeir
Dubh
perch

2

2

5

⊥

7

LOCH

pier

FR

4

2

Coll

■ Arivirig

⊥

2

+

Eilean
Eatharna

3

⊥

2

+

Eilean
Dubh

Meall
Eatharna
▲

perch McQuarry's Rock

EATHARNA

½

+

+

Bogha Mor

▲ fl 6 secs.

6

←— 2 cables —→

left Looking down on the narrows in Loch Teachdais from above Rahoy House
Metal-green sea off the Treshnish Isles

When the tide turned the wind strengthened even more and we had had enough, particularly as the lights of the hotel were clearly visible on the hill. Trevor pulled in the anchors and, using the engine to hold her head to wind, we allowed *Hebe* to slip back until she was level with the pier. One flat-out blast of the six horses and the small boat struggled into the shelter of the old stonework. It was last light and the Germans in their Bismark of a boat watched with pale, envious faces as we strolled towards the pub.

The hotel at Arinagour is a friendly place full of unexpected facilities such as a sauna bath. It is run by Alistair Oliphant, formerly a conjuror from Glasgow. The island has a population of fewer than 150, most of whom live in or near the town. The rest of Coll is low and lunar-like. A new pier was built in 1969 but is often busy with ferries and fishing boats. Coll is about 12 miles long by 3 miles wide and has a west coast of white sand bays. Being low-lying it does not generate cloudy weather. A road west from Arinagour leads to Breachacha Castle, home of the Macleans of Coll until 1750 when the then chieftain, Hector Maclean, built a much less imposing castle a short walk away. Dr. Johnson saw this building and dismissed it as 'a mere tradesman's box'. The turrets and parapet were cosmetic features added in the nineteenth century. The new castle is being turned into flats and the old castle restored by young people under the direction of the Project Trust.

Coll suffered slow depopulation over the years after the clearances. Since 1964 a large part of the island has been owned by a Dutchman, Jan de Vries, the head of a multi-national building and civil engineering organisation, whose main aim is directed at the island's pheasant and partridge.

The highest point on the island, Ben Hogh, is only 395 ft. high but gives a fine view across the Minch to the Outer Hebrides. Coll is an island with peace, quietness and some superb beaches as its main assets. Since these are precisely what most visitors seek, all is well. There are shops near the pier and in the grass beyond a cleverly concealed water tap.

Skate

Arinagour, Coll

The Atlantic beats against the west coast of Mull with a strong, relentless rhythm. It is a fine coast with high mountains and a craggy, deserted shoreline. *Hebe* made good progress in the wake of the previous day's storm which had stirred the sea into a huge rolling swell that swallowed the Caledonian MacBrayne ferry crossing ahead of us, leaving only the tip of her funnel showing. The next second the whole ship would be disgorged from masthead to plimsoll line.

GOMETRA

Map ref. 6B4
Water (well, west shore)

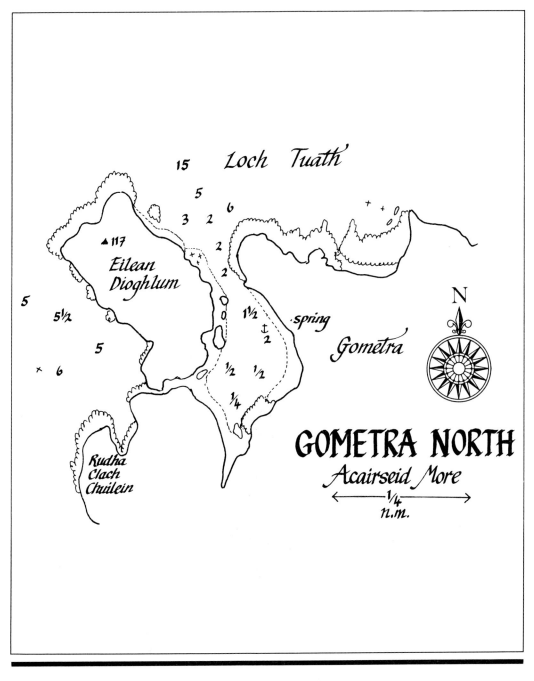

Guillemot. Breeds in dense colonies on narrow cliff ledges; the female lays one egg on the bare rock

During the morning warm weather returned and as it arrived so the wind died. The Treshnish Islands lay astern like a flotilla of aircraft carriers and the sea as we neared the shelter of Loch Tuath turned into a gently tilting sheet of glass. Limp sails were furled and the engine spluttered into life. Around *Hebe's* wake the sea was a tropical blue with a fine summer haze about it. How astonishing that the weather could change so dramatically in the space of a couple of hours. We slipped into north Gometra anchorage, steering well to the east shore in the narrow entrance. It is one of the most perfect in the Hebrides; an almost land-locked pool where a boat might weather the worst storm. The sun was scorching. Trevor dipped a bottle of Bull's Blood into the cooling waters on the end of a length of line. It was around here that John McLintock, author of *West Coast Cruising,* considered what yachtsmen meant when they talked about 'snug' anchorages. 'To be really snug,' he wrote, 'let me be in the small cabin of a small yacht during heavy weather, and put between my boat and me and the leaping seas a small islet or two, just a few acres of sturdy rock, so that I may sit back in warm contentment and hear not only the whining rigging and the swishing rain, but also the loud thunders of the breakers round the corner. *That* is snugness'.

It was easy to imagine McLintock relishing the snugness behind Eilean Dioghlum as the Atlantic exploded against the western edge of the island. Today however the pool was a flat blue disc resembling a Pacific lagoon. A couple of mackerel were sizzling beneath the grill and the bottle was towed up from the cool depths. Improper to chill a bottle of bra' bodied red, you say? It was a hot day.

The snug shelter of Gometra North

There is an admirable compactness about a small, well-found cruiser. Within the span of a few feet there is everything necessary for total independence. A man can fetch up to a port or island and liking the look of it, stay. If not, he can up anchor and move on to somewhere more attractive; the free-ranging choice of the sea-borne nomad.

We wanted to stay on Staffa, that most extraordinary island, but we were not totally confident that the weather would hold fair overnight. Already there were huge armadas of milky clouds billowing in from west-south-west and signs above them of strong colder winds in the lingering veil of alto-cirrus.

STAFFA

Map ref. 7B5
No facilities

West Coast, Staffa

A good wind had brought *Hebe* on one long fetch from Gometra, riding the steady swell until, in the lea of the island, the anchor disappeared into a jungle growth of kelp. The two-man inflatable seemed too frail a craft to approach the normal landing stage. The swell was hammering in by the iron railing marking the place and turning to angry white foam. Instead, we landed on a beach of richly-coloured and sea-smoothed pebbles almost opposite Cormorant Cave.

Staffa is less than half a mile long and was first 'discovered' in August 1722 by the botanist Sir Joseph Banks, who had accompanied Captain Cook as chief scientist on his first voyage round the world on board the *Endeavour*. Banks was impressed by 'a scene of magnificence which exceeded our expectations' when he saw the tall cliffs of columnar basalt and the fantastic natural architecture of the island. A geological description by him was published and Staffa's fame secured. A long line of authors and artists including Scott, Keats, Wordsworth, Tennyson, Turner and Jules Verne visited and wrote about the island. But it was Banks who named the great cave in the southern cliffs after Fingal, father of the legendary Ossian. In storm conditions the pressure of the sea against the cave mouth creates a loud compressed booming noise and it was probably this sound that inspired Mendelssohn to write his Hebridean Overture, also known as Fingal's Cave. It was to him 'like the interior of a gigantic organ for the winds and tumultuous waves to play on'. Dr Johnson and Boswell sailed past the island but were not impressed.

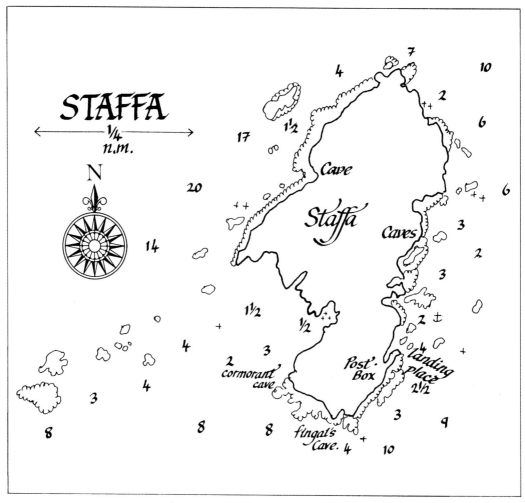

The remarkable hexagonal columns of basalt that give the look of a rugged stockade to the southern and western cliffs were formed by a particular pattern in the cooling of molten lava associated with volcanic activity. The island has been uninhabited for two centuries except for sheep who are the only permanent residents, grazing the rolling cap of grass that stretches to the edge of the cliffs. Near the landing stage is a post box where cards and letters may be posted to be franked with a special Staffa stamp. Staffa has a particular magic with its spectacular rocks, rowdy birdlife and the incessant noise of the sea brushing against it.

We were able to work *Hebe,* with her shallow draught, into calm water off the beach south of Goat Cave, but the rocks outlying the east side of Mull make this more hazardous for larger yachts. The safest approach is from the south-east, keeping Erisgeir astern and the landing place with its steps on the bow. The anchorage in about 4 fathoms has foul ground on both sides and should only be approached in calm weather. West Coast cruising devotees may have to wait patiently through several seasons before the chance comes to land on Staffa.

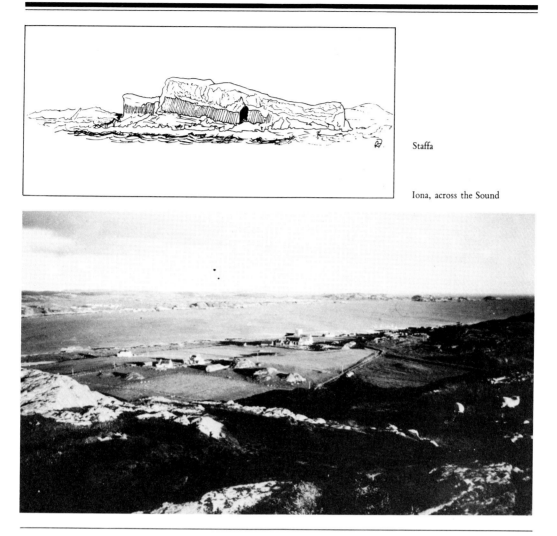

Staffa

Iona, across the Sound

'Tricky bit, this one,' Trevor said, watching the sand slip by unnervingly close to the keels and scouring chart 2617 for a deeper passage. He could not find an obvious one and concluded that the Sound of Iona was not a place to be in a yacht on the descending spring side. We kept well clear of the Mull shore which sends out a number of obstacles and followed ecclesiastical landmarks - the Cathedral and the Free Church - to an anchorage just south of the slipway off the Bay of the Martyrs. The whole width of the sound between the landing on Iona and Fionnphort is severely shoal and requires careful navigation.

There was a windy sky as we settled at anchor. On the summit of Dun I, the highest point of the island, someone was flying a kite that danced wildly about the sky showing that conditions on the weather shore of Iona would be quite wild. The squat tower of the Cathedral stood solidly above the cluster of rooftops, marking the historical importance of the island. It was here that St. Columba landed from Ireland in AD 563 and began the spread of Christianity in the west and north of Scotland.

IONA

Map ref. 7B5
Hotels and services.
Fionnphort (Mull):
water, shop, PO

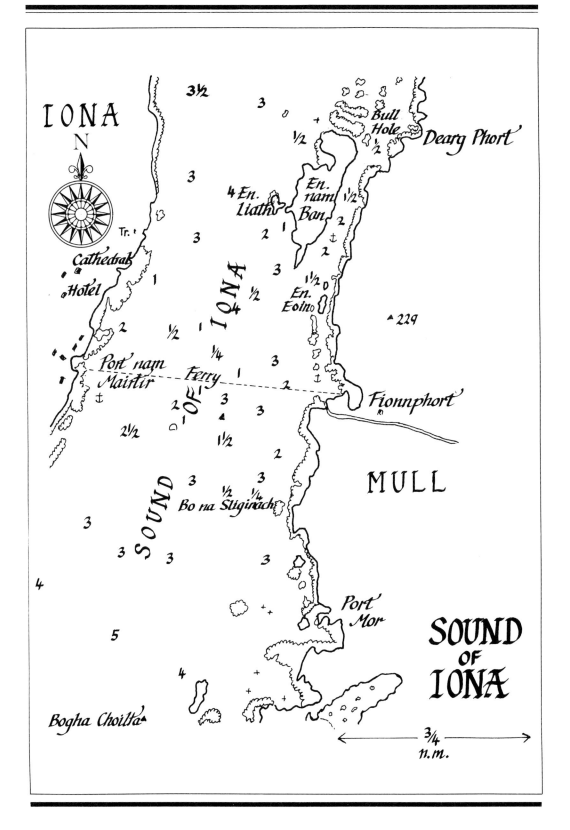

Iona Cathedral

The place is one of pilgrimage for the faithful and now rests in the guardianship of the National Trust for Scotland. More than half a million visitors a year come to the island, tramping the half mile separating the jetty and the Cathedral which has been finely restored. Iona is an island of kings, the crucible of the Celtic kingdom of Scotland. It was here that Aidan of Dalriada, the first king in the history of Britain, was consecrated, and by one estimate the burial ground at Reilig Odhrain contains the graves of forty-eight Scottish, eight Norwegian and four Irish kings.

Dr. Johnson, unimpressed by the natural grandeur of Staffa, stranded on the horizon to the north, had more feeling for Iona. That man was little to be envied whose piety did not grow warmer among the ruins of Iona, he declared.

Next to the burial ground is the stark granite chapel of St. Oran, said to have been rebuilt in the eleventh century on the site of a much earlier chapel. Other enduring signs of Iona's foundation include the huge cross near the west door of the Cathedral that has stood where it was carved for more than a thousand years.

The Cathedral is run by the Iona Community, whose members ensure that a continuing thread of worship and Christian activity continues, and was given in trust to the Church of Scotland in 1912. The quiet spirit of Iona survives the tourism the island inevitably attracts, as it survived the savage raids from Norse and pagan invasions that followed Columba's death.

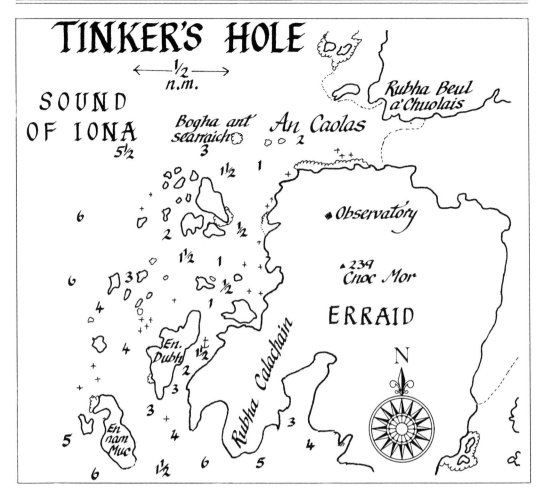

Tinker's Hole, Sound of Iona.
Well sheltered from wind, but
feels the flow of the tide.

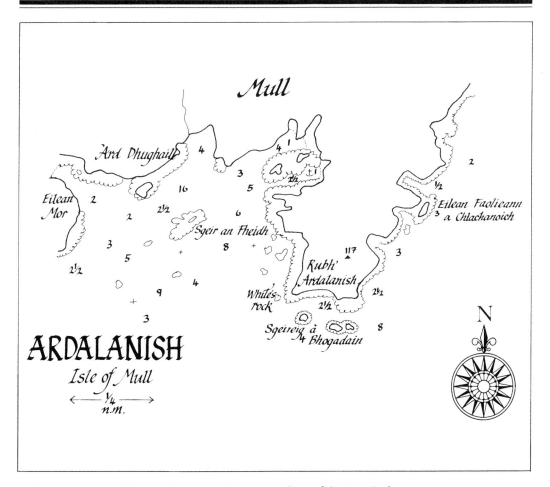

Mull

Ard Dhughaill 4 4 1

3 2½ ‡ 1

Eilean 2 16 5 ½ 2

Mor 2 2½ 6 *Eilean Faolieann*

3 *a Chlachanoich*

3 *Sgeir an Fheidh*

5 8 + 117 3

2½ 9 4 *Rubh'*

+ *Ardalanish*

3 *White's* 2½

rock 2½ 8

Sgeireig à

N

Bhogadain

ARDALANISH

Isle of Mull

←— ¼ —→

n.m.

There are two excellent anchorages on the eastern shore of the Sound of Iona; Bull Hole behind Eilean nam Ban and Tinker's Hole off the west shore of Erraid. Both give excellent shelter. *Hebe* entered Bull Hole after passing to the north of the foul ground in the Sound, then following the tip of pinky rock marking the southern point of Eilean nam Ban. Holding the centre channel the passage was clear to the open pool of the Bull Hole itself, occupied that day by a reserve ferry and a scattering of other small craft.

Tinker's Hole was the perfect place for a small yacht but trickier to reach. With Trevor keeping watch over the bow and with a full tide under the keel we felt our way in from the north, heading directly for the dome of the disused observatory on Erraid, over a shallow patch south of Eilean Ghòmain and down through the islets and rocks to the north of Eilean Dubh. A deeper-draught vessel would be wise to approach from the Sound of Iona by leaving the islands and rocks guarding the Tinker's Hole to port and entering the anchorage from the south. It is a snug, rock-sheltered place with firm holding ground but open to swell and strong winds from the south and affected by strong tides that can channel through Tinker's Hole like an embryo millrace.

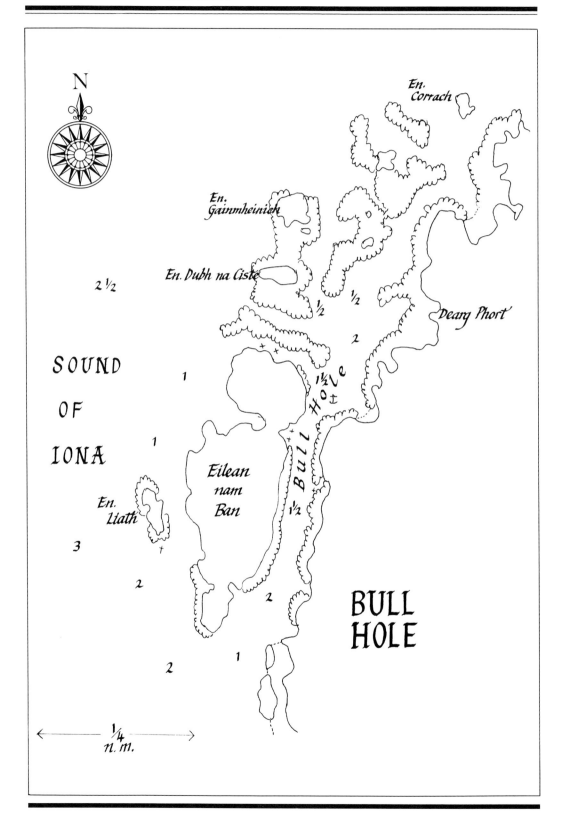

N

En. Corrach

En. Gainmheinich

En. Dubh na Ciste

2 ½

½

½

Dearg Phort

2

1

SOUND

OF

IONA

Bull Hole

1½

1

En. Liath

Eilean nam Ban

3

½

1½

2

2

2

1

BULL HOLE

¼
n. m.

Our exploration of this delectable corner of Mull that fine August day ended at a true gem of an anchorage, Ardalanish. The 4-mile passage from Erraid along the rock-bound coast was tremendously exciting. The sea, a deep Pacific blue that turned to sparkling silver on the horizon, surged with a subdued power against Rankin's Rocks and Sgeir na Caillich, occasionally exploding in a white froth of spray. *Hebe* scurried along under full sail, a gentle sou'westerly wind pushing her at the fastest point of sailing to the landward side of Livingston's Rocks and round a broken headland that brought Rubh' Ardalanish into view on the port bow. The entrance was more difficult with high water sweeping round Sgeir an Fheidh and almost covering the cluster of rocks to the east, but a compass course holding the entrance at 035° took *Hebe* goose-winged into the perfect shelter of the anchorage. It was a true coastal wilderness with warm, grey rocks dotted with scrub, clear water and the anchor chain curving through 4 fathoms to a sandy bed. Trevor extricated a couple of large chops that had been lurking in the cold box for a few days, sniffed at them, declared they were fit for human consumption and soon the perfection was completed by the smell of sizzling lamb and mint sauce.

Coal-fish or Saithe

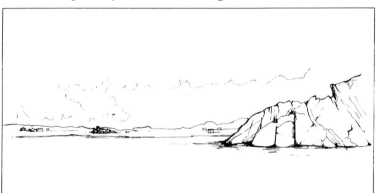

Entrance to Bull Hole

Bull Hole, Sound of Iona

SANNA BAY

Map ref. 6C2
Water (tap by cottages),
PO, inn 3m; avoid in westerlies
because of strong swell setting
into the bay

Merlin. Usually nests in
heather; commonly winters
in coastal areas and estuaries;
predatory

Ardnamurchan Point is a terror for some; a harsh, black finger pointing into a confusion of sea, 'breakfast point' for boats heading north from Tobermory that hit the sickening swell after an early start. Our first trip around this deadly headland held no terrors. It was a burning hot day, there was not a breath of wind, the sea was flat as a billiard table and our engine stubbornly refused to work. After the ritual dismantling and reassembly and still without sign of life, we abandoned hope of power and began to tow *Hebe* with the dinghy. Slowly, the headland slipped by, the rocks only a few feet away. 'Some Cape Horn of the West, this!' Trevor remarked, pulling on the slender plastic oars and making the dinghy snatch at *Hebe's* bow.

The lighthouse stood tall and irrelevant on the point as *Hebe* crept by. It took hours to pull the boat, taking turns at the oars, to round the headland and cover the 1¼ miles to Sanna Bay, the most convenient anchorage to Ardnamurchan. In southerly winds there is a snug anchorage at Sanna Bay, half an hour's sail beyond the lighthouse; a broad circle of sand and reefs well-protected from the worst of the weather. Although wide-mouthed, the Bay demands care principally from the reef which runs from the hills above the village and from a string of individual rocks which dot the north shore. We picked out the wide beach which is the first seaward mark and headed in with the early flood towards the shore, still some ¾ mile away. Through glasses we noted the water tower, not a perfect mark since it tended to blend into the hill behind and as the shore closed, disappeared altogether behind the bulk of the north shore. The line of the reef, marked by a dark stain of seaweed, appeared abruptly but we cleared it and slipped into a quiet lagoon. When to turn? The water tower had disappeared and we had to guess its position but there was the building with two red doors. Had the Clyde Cruising Club supplied the farmer with a job lot of red paint to ensure a consistent mark? What happened if the farmer left his door open? The vision of a line of disorientated yachtsmen wandering onto reefs simply because a farmer wanted to get his tractor out sprang to mind. A couple of cables from the beach we let the anchor go into a fathom or more of crystal clear water. We watched it descend like a bomb and strike a patch of sand squarely. *Hebe* swung gently round head to wind.

Ardnamurchan Point

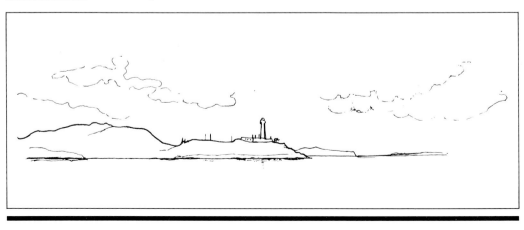

There is a Post Office ashore, water from a tap beside one of the cottages and an excellent pub about 3 miles down the road towards Kilchoan. The beaches around Sanna are superb and in fine weather this is an idyllic anchorage for doing nothing more than stretching out on warm sand in total solitude.

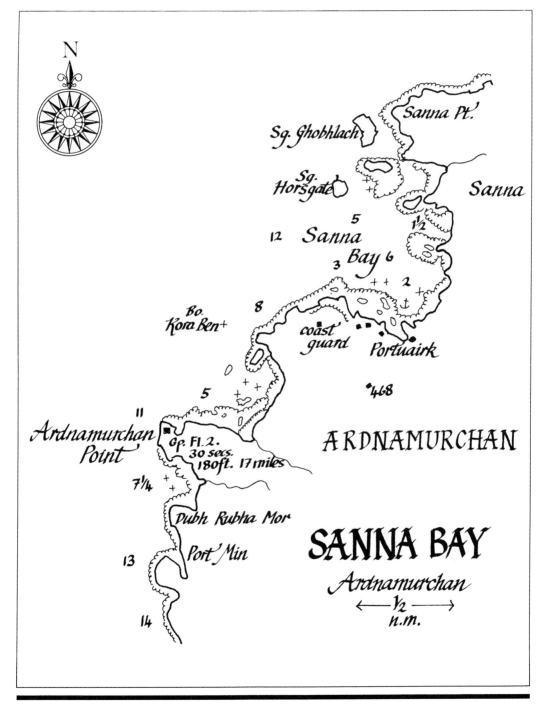

THE SMALL ISLES

Map ref. 13A7 - 6C2

Cormorant. Nests on wide ledges and rocky islets; feeds on fish. Some individuals wander as far as Spain

Sanna Bay

Few parts of the West give greater variety and a sense of open sailing than an exploration of the Small Isles, those quaintly named islands Muck, Eigg, Rhum and Canna. Each one is totally different from its neighbour; Muck lies low and fertile, farmed to its very edges; Eigg rises from the sea like an island in the South Pacific, Rhum is a place of high mountain ridges, a miniature Cuillins divided from Skye by the 7 miles of Cuillin Sound. Tucked away behind Rhum is the delectable gem of Canna with its bird cliffs and superb anchorage between the main island and the satellite of Sanday.

We left Sanna for an exploration of the Small Isles just as the weather broke. The departure was spectacular. The engine refused to work and we had anchored the previous evening at high water well into the shelter of the reef that protects the western entrance of Sanna Bay. During the night the wind had swung south of east and was bellowing across the bay, pushing *Hebe* taut on her anchor warp. The tide had also departed so that the small yacht's stern was no more than ten yards from the reef. The rocks had lost their protective appearance and had more the look of snapping teeth. Trevor took in the position when he stuck his head out of the hatch. The wind was forecast to strengthen later, still from the east. We could not let *Hebe* lie further back on her anchor and if she dragged she would be onto the rocks in a trice. We could not sail her off because of her graceful habit of swooping to leeward before picking up way into the wind.

A gust of wind gave the halyards an irritated rattle, demanding action. *Hebe* was beginning to ride the swell building up against the reef. Down went the dinghy. We laid a kedge as far out into the bay as possible, set the sails and hauled in both anchor warps. *Hebe* moved away from the rocks but even with more searoom she would have to sail away on a port tack to avoid them. The sails filled, the leeward swoop was checked, the two anchors came up smoothly and *Hebe* sailed unruffled into clear water. As she went about onto starboard, we passed a Ballad anchored sensibly clear of the rocks and got a round of applause from a couple on board who had been watching our manoueuvres. Sometimes on a sailing boat things happen with a marvellous precision. Sometimes.

Muck is the smallest of the Small Isles. The name does not derive from any look of scruffiness and Muck by any other name would be as delightful, fertile and industrious. The word is most likely a corruption of the Gaelic muc-mahara, meaning sea-pig or porpoise. It was an odd embarrassment to the island's laird in the days when Highland protocol insisted that a man be addressed by the name of his lands. Muck prospered in the Napoleonic wars when the islanders laboriously harvested the kelp washed onto the shore which they dried and turned into potash, an ingredient of gunpowder. In the nineteenth century the island, which had supported about 300 people, was cleared. Families were evicted and obliged to sail for the New World, most of them settling in Nova Scotia and on Cape Breton Island. Muck, like its inner Hebridean neighbours, never recovered but the present owners are trying hard to ensure their small community has a future.

MUCK

Map ref. 6C2
Water, shop, PO;
avoid Gallanach Bay
in northerlies

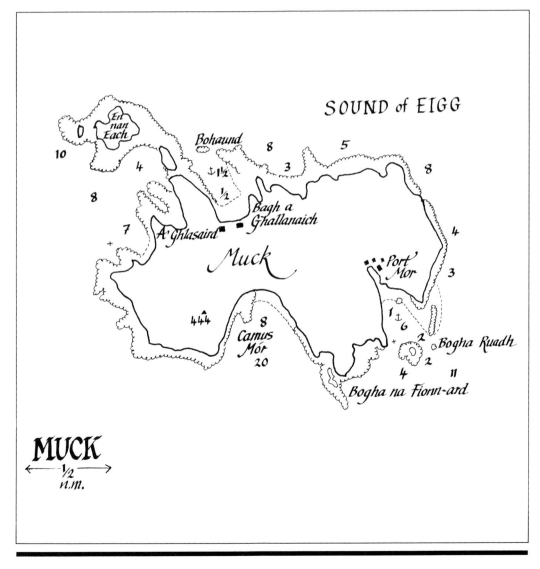

The MacEwen brothers inherited the island and farm it very productively, using every foot of the fertile, volcanic soil. There are 1,600 acres of Muck of which 100 are cultivated and the rest high quality pasture. The island's prosperity has always relied on the enterprise of the owners and the MacEwens have developed cattle farming, pony breeding and some tourism as a way of bringing Muck as close as possible to self-sufficiency. They think in terms of a collective in which the islanders would each contribute their skills and add their energy towards making the island a viable community.

There are two anchorages. Port Mor lies on the south-east side of the island and gives good shelter when the wind lies in the north or west. Entry is made in between the Bogha Ruadh, which is awash at low water springs, and the long reef of Dubhsgeir. There is good holding ground in 4 fathoms about 1 cable from the stone pier. Gallanach Bay (Bagh a Ghallanaich) is the anchorage in the north and requires care because the entrance is obstructed with rocks, notably the Bohaund which shows two dark heads at low water springs. This anchorage should not be approached in northerly winds because a bad swell sets into the bay. Pass either side of the Bohaund. The west passage is deeper but is threatened by a long spit running out to Eilean nan Each. There is a great variety of birdlife nesting in the rocks to the north-west of the anchorage and a good beach. Occasionally the Atlantic drift washes up beans from the West Indies that are looked on as lucky charms.

Gallanach Bay

Eigg rocked gently on the steady swell, the low evening light catching the tip of the Sgurr and etching the clear outline of the lazy beds, the overgrown agricultural plots west of Galmisdale. The tropical island-look that the high sugar loaf of the Sgurr gives to Eigg is reinforced by the palm trees and bamboo that grow in the gardens of the Lodge, a colonial-style residence half a mile from the pier. The wind was back in the west and the slack water between Eilean Castle and the main island was flat calm. We rounded the island, motoring between the two perches that mark foul ground and anchoring in shallow water short of the pier. This could be a difficult place for deep-draught boats; the alternatives being the deeper water south of the jetty, which is exposed to south-west winds, or good holding ground behind Eilean Castle and the reef Garbh Sgeir.

Eigg was known in ancient times as Eilean Ninban More or the Isle of the Big Women and with this piece of information freshly culled from a guide book we were startled to be greeted at the pier by a beautiful, tall woman. She was not descended from the tribe of Amazons who slaughtered the good monk St. Duncan and his followers in the seventh century after they had tried some over-zealous missionary work on Eigg. This lady was a daughter of Mr. Keith Schellenberg, the present laird of Eigg, and she ran the island's tea room which sells home baking but not egg sandwiches.

EIGG

Map ref. 6C1
Water, shop, PO

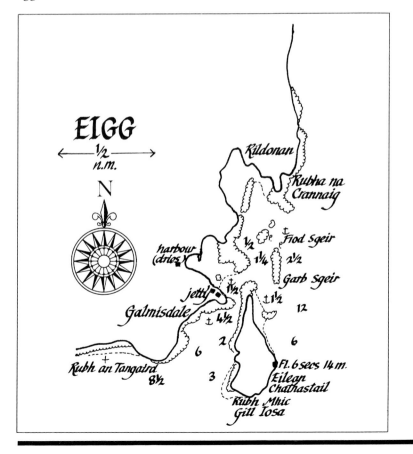

Eigg harbour

Manx Shearwater. Breeds in colonies on rocky islands off west coast; feeds on plankton

Mr. Schellenberg is another energetic landowner keen to turn his lovely island into a thriving, profitable community. He runs a private ferry to and from the mainland and once proposed that all the Small Isles should be serviced by a private enterprise ferry, instead of the state-owned Caledonian MacBrayne. This idea was not happily received by his more exposed neighbours. The MacEwens of Muck commented that 'Mr Schellenberg is temporal, Caledonian MacBrayne are eternal'.

This is a large and beautiful island with a long ridge running from Beinn Tigh to the Sgurr and another forming a curving northerly arm ending in Dunan Thalasgair. The Sgurr is a 400 ft.-high knot of pitchstone and in other parts of the island the same hexagonal columns of basalt can be found that erupt so spectacularly on Staffa.

There are many caves in the southern cliffs, one with a particularly gory piece of history attached to it. The story goes that in the winter of 1577 some Macleods from Skye raided the island and raped or assaulted (the stories differ) some of the Macdonald of Eigg girls. The Macleods were caught, castrated and sent back to Skye. 'Justice' was demanded. The Macleod chief launched a fleet of galleys carrying a powerful force of men. The Macdonalds realized they were outnumbered and retreated to the Cave of Francis, a deep grotto with a small, well-hidden entrance. After three days in hiding a scout was sent out but the Macleods were still searching the island and followed his footprints in the snow back to the cave. They lit a bonfire at the entrance and asphyxiated the 400 islanders hiding inside. It was only in the last century that the bones were removed to the ruins of the island's ancient chapel.

Eigg now has a population of 80, although that number increases sharply in the summer season when the holiday bungalows - one of them an old water mill - fill up. There are fewer than 20 telephones but the island boasts a new 100-line £100,000 automatic telephone exchange. Perhaps the Post Office expects a population boom on Eigg!

The island has a minibus service that takes visitors across the low valley to Cleadale. Near Camus Sgiotaig are the singing sands, so-called because the white quartz beach squeaks underfoot, and moans when a strong wind stirs the ground. When we were there the forecast announced that Force 10 winds were approaching for sea area Hebrides. Mares' tails streaked the sky and the lower clouds looked ragged and bruised. At high water we slid behind the old pier beyond the jetty and snugged in against the old stone. As the wind strengthened the tide departed and *Hebe* sat comfortably on her keels whilst outside yachtsmen nervously watched their anchors and one unfortunate was actually blown aground. Being small and double-keeled is an advantage sometimes.

Rhum is a natural laboratory for geology, biology, ornithology and a variety of other natural sciences. Since the Maclean of Coll packed off the native population by boat to Nova Scotia in 1828, the island has been a restricted area, privately owned. The rambling sandstone castle at Kinloch was built by Sir George Bullough, heir to a Lancashire mill-owner, and is an outrageous example of Edwardian opulence. The castle is now an hotel run by the National Trust for Scotland and the island is owned by the Nature Conservancy Council. It is an important centre for red deer research and for recording an undisturbed environment. Visitors are asked to check with the Warden before venturing away from Loch Scresort where the only safe anchorage is to be found. Rhum offers few facilities but is well worth a call. There are two nature trails running along the south side of the loch and up Kinloch Glen.

RHUM

Map ref. 13C8
Kinloch: water, shop, PO; exposed in easterlies

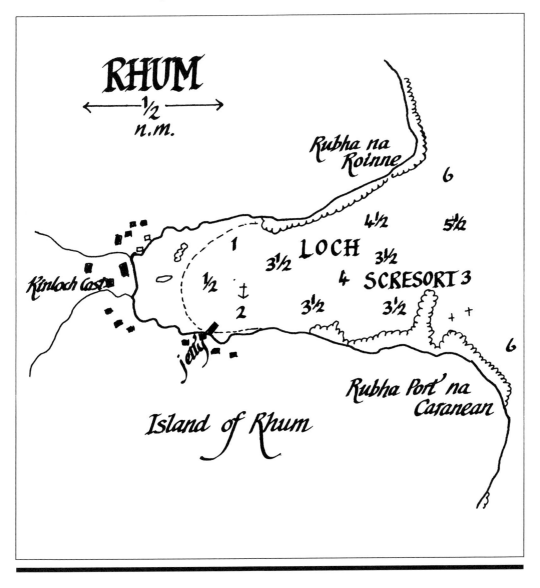

Rhum has wild goats, large herds of red deer, its own long-tailed field mice, and an impressive population of moths and butterflies. There are Highland cattle and the Rhum ponies (traditionally associated with the Spanish Armada and the Vikings) that are used to carry down deer carcasses culled on the hill. Few places can have had such a careful inventory made of every species of bird and insect resident. Most remarkable is the colony of Manx shearwaters, some 70,000 breeding pairs strong, that nest in mountain-top burrows on Trollaval Peak, the peak of the Trolls. Nowhere else in Britain do the birds nest in such a curious place, making a weird nocturnal din and on instinct abandoning the chicks before they can fly, leaving them to make their own way 1,500 ft to the sea.

There are volcanic rocks of a form found only on Rhum and the moon; and fine walks between Allival and Askival and among the group of Nordic-sounding mountains on the southern point of the island. They are a reminder that Rhum only became part of the Scottish kingdom in 1266. Before then it was dominated by Norway.

The interior of the island is magnificently barren. Glen Harris has a fine raised beach near the point where the Bulloughs lie buried beneath a large mausoleum built in the style of a Greek temple.

Sir George, son of the Bullough who acquired the estate in 1871, ordered the construction of the castle at the turn of the century. The red sandstone was shipped from Arran and the soil for the gardens brought from Ayrshire. The workmen from the Bullough's home county, Lancashire, were fitted out with kilts and they turned Rhum into a private estate with hydro-electric power and a 'castle' with air conditioning, elegantly furnished rooms and what is now the only orchestrion in working order. Properly primed, this 'busker's dream', as one observer described it, can still blast out the music that kept the Bulloughs and their guests entertained.

Loch Scresort is well sheltered in anything but easterly winds and is clear except for a bad reef stretching for two cables from the southern point of the entrance. The jetty is on the south shore but deep-draught boats should anchor well off in 3 fathoms. Some provisions are available and there is a telephone at Kinloch Post Office. Water should be taken from the burn near the pier.

Kinloch Castle, Loch Scresort, Rhum

Around the shoulder of Rhum and resting on the horizon like a whale lies the last of the Small Isles but not the least. Canna has yet another distinct character and history, another one-man island until recently when the laird, the historian and naturalist John Lorne Campbell, handed his treasured property to the care of the National Trust for Scotland. Dr. Campbell has owned the island since 1938 and became a convert both to Catholicism and gaeldom. The island is his farm where pedigree highland cattle and fearsomely horned pedigree rams are bred. Canna is linked by a bridge to Sanday and the stretch of water in the crook between them is one of the finest anchorages in the west. I have waited comfortably in Canna harbour whilst the sea outside in Canna Sound turned into a boiling stretch of foam-streaked water. In the days of sail the harbour was the midway port for vessels trading between the mainland and the Outer Isles.

CANNA

Map ref. 13B7
Water and some provisions at farm, PO

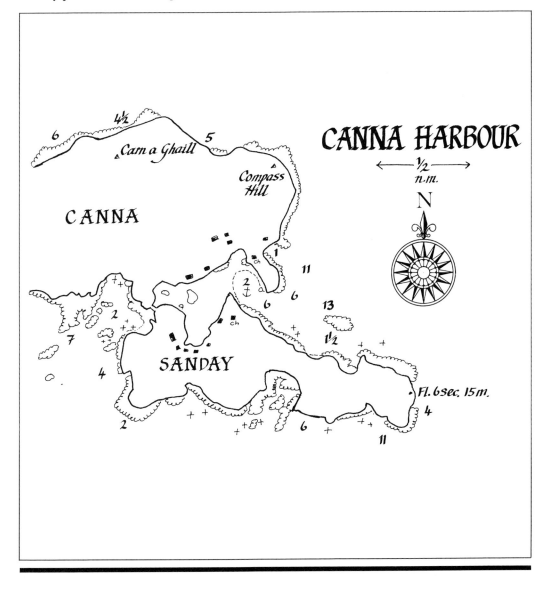

Canna Harbour

On stormy winter days many a fleet of luggers, gabbarts and smacks rode out the gale. The popularity of Canna harbour may be judged by the graffiti scrawled and chipped into the harbour wall near the pier. Those were the days when the islands had a population big enough to support three churches, but now there are only 23 living on the island, and Sanday, which had a population of more than 100 pre-war, is deserted. The island has always held to the 'old religion' and the Catholic population now worships in the small chapel near the Post Office. The Church of Scotland built a kirk in the style of the early Celtic churches with a conical bell tower. It is kept watertight by visiting worker-ministers but is not often used. The principal house on the island is Canna House, home of Dr. Campbell and his wife, the American writer Margaret Fay Shaw. They have both been devoted to recording the history of the Hebrides and to working practically to improve the economy. Dr. Campbell was one of the moving spirits behind the Highlands and Islands Development Board, the government agency charged with improving the economic prospects for the region.

Graffitti on the rocks at Canna harbour

The island is about 5 miles long by 1 mile wide and the western cliffs are a superb bird sanctuary. Dr. Campbell refuses to allow the thistles on the island to be cut because they are an essential source of food for certain species of butterfly and moth. The tiny community is served by a Post Office supervised by Post Mistress Mary Ann MacLean, a native of Canna, by a telephone kiosk and by peripatetic priests, doctors and piano tuners (the Small Isles have between them two Steinways and a Bechstein).

Only at dead high water in an easterly gale is Canna harbour at all exposed and even then the swell is more uncomfortable then dangerous. A patch of rocks impedes a direct approach to the harbour mouth and the best course is to arrive off Ru Cirenish from the north-east, head for the church on Sanday until the pair of cottages on the shore are in line with the cottage beyond and then turn into the harbour. This course should avoid a patch of rock off the pier. For best shelter anchor towards the Canna shore in 2 fathoms.

LOCH SCAVAIG

Map ref. 13C6
No facilities

The rugged Cuillin mountains fall into the sea behind Loch Scavaig, the grandest anchorage on the west coast. The steep slopes brooding over this sheltered cove are one of the greatest hazards. Squalls may avalanche down them when the wind is from the north and in such conditions it is wise to run a line ashore. The holding ground is soft mud and suspect. My 'companion' John McLintock found the place impressive. 'Scavaig is one of the darkest frowns on the coast face of Skye. From the tops of the sawn-off cliffs past which we had been sailing, the land slopes inland to the hills.

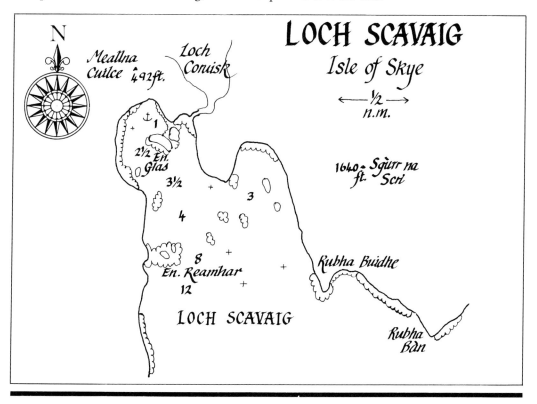

But at Scavaig the hills are the coast. The Cuillin giants come striding down there to the ocean, and stand brooding in grim and solemn watchfulness over the dark blue waters of the loch. In the sombre shadows of their presence a yacht becomes a pigmy thing. And if you drop anchor behind Eilean Glas at the head of the loch, and follow the brawling waters of the Mad Burn till you stand on that rock ledge with Scavaig behind you and the awful solitude of Loch Coruisk in front, it will be strange if you do not find your voice reducing to an awed whisper, and in your heart a feeling of the insignificance of man in the presence of the Great Primordial. But I refuse to attempt to describe this place'.

Just as well. In settled weather, Scavaig is an excellent base from which to explore the Cuillin ridge or the lonely reaches of Loch Coruisk which empties into Scavaig.

The approach is towards the western shore of the loch. We gave Eilean Reamhar a clear berth, heading directly for Eilean Glas. It was nearly low water and a calm day so that all the hazards were standing out clearly. *Hebe* crept up the loch, edging to port as the shoal patch of Sgeir Doghigh slipped by and we could identify Eilean Glas. There were 2 fathoms of dark, peat-stained water and then a clear patch of sand showed through in the 60-yard gap between the island and a line of bad rocks immediately to the west.

ISLE ORNSAY

Map ref. 13E7
Water (tap and well)
hotel, PO

This is a good port of call for embryo Gaelic-speakers to come and practise. The hotel is run by Mr. Iain Noble, who is himself mastering the language and is an active campaigner on behalf of Gaelic culture. It is a friendly, informal place with an unusual bar in that pipers are apt to wheeze into life and slow march around the room, rattling the dart board with a blare of pibroch. The food is excellent and baths are available. In the days of sail the bay between Isle Ornsay and the Skye shore would be deck to deck with fishing boats; now it is only cruising craft and the occasional workboat that come in. The bay beyond the building dries out for a long way and the surest anchorage is south of a line drawn between the low cliffs running from the north-west point of the island and the light beacon beyond.

Isle Ornsay

ISLE ORNSAY
Isle of Skye

SKYE

N

Isleomsay

Hotel

cliff

Ornsay

Fl.R 6 secs.
26 f. 4 m.

En. Sionnach
Gp.Fl. 2. 7secs.
60ft. 12m.

Ard Ghunel

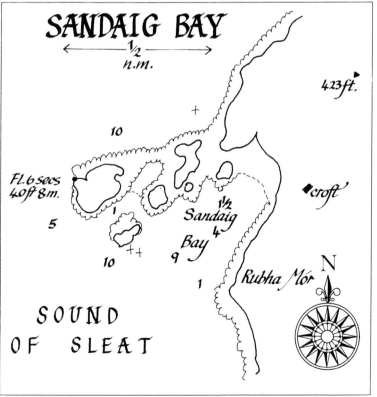

SANDAIG BAY

Fl. 6 secs
40ft 8m.

Sandaig
Bay

croft

423ft.

Rubha Mór

N

SOUND
OF SLEAT

SANDAIG

Map ref. 13F6
No facilities; avoid
in south-westerlies

Gales were forecast for Malin and Hebrides and cloud was already building up in the west. The passage from Isle Ornsay to Sandaig was 3½ miles and the plan was to anchor there to wait for low water at Kyle Rhea just after noon. The wind was blowing directly into Sandaig Bay and had built the sea into a lumpy, dark swell that had the full send of the Sound of Sleat behind it. The sea surged in slightly at an angle and I hoped for some shelter behind the rocks that ran from Sandaig Island light. Inside the reef the sea eased a little but it was still uncomfortable and with stronger winds forecast I skirted across the rollers parallel with the pebble beach opposite this lonely place that had strong associations with the author Gavin Maxwell. I beat out into the Sound of Sleat without even trying to put down the anchor. A note in the log: 'Enter Sandaig Bay 12.10, depart 12.17. Must come back!' Even so the idea was sound in a short waterline bilge-keeler like *Hebe*. There is no merit in flogging a fast foul ebb-tide for hours when a spell at anchor for a meal in comfort waiting for the flood puts you only half an hour behind at the end of the day.

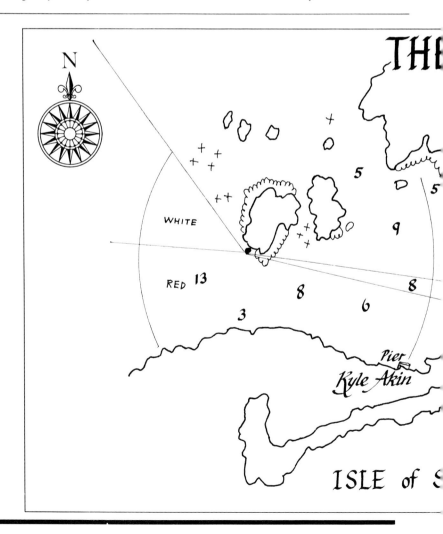

This is an important point for west coast cruising yachts. It is a good centre for re-stocking or re-fuelling although piers and jetties may be busy
with ferries, oil-industry ships and Royal Navy vessels. In calm weather
there is temporary anchorage off the Kyle of Lochalsh Hotel but in bad
conditions, particularly strong westerly winds, the best shelter is in Loch
na Beist, the Loch of the Bear, on the Skye shore, which has good holding
ground. The loch lies ¾-mile east of Kyleakin and is a good place to wait
for a favourable tide through the Kyle Rhea narrows. Cailleach anchorage
on the Skye shore just north of Sgeir na Cailleach beacon is also a convenient place to wait for the tide and ponder on the thought that Haakon also
waited there for the southerly ebb with his fleet on the way to do
battle with Alexander III at Largs.

The passage between Kyle and the Inner Sound requires care and timing. Skye and the mainland are separated by a channel 2 cables wide at
Kyle Rhea and the spring ebb attains 8 knots. If the rush of water meets
strong southerly winds off Glenelg, a ferocious sea may develop. It is best

KYLE OF LOCHALSH

Map ref. 13E6
All facilities

Gannet. Nests in colo-
nies on rocky islands and
stacks; young birds mi-
grate until mature

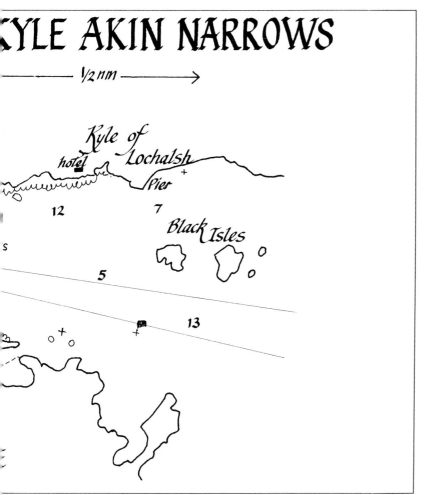

to wait for slack water, a time when in olden days herds of cattle driven from Skye to the lowland markets were swum across the Kyle roped tail to muzzle in batches of five astern of the ferry boat.

John McLintock clearly did not time his passage through Kyle Rhea quite accurately, although his makes the most dramatic description. 'The flood had us already in its irresistible clutch. We seemed to be speeding into a dead-end, hemmed in by heather hills. Soon, however, there opened out, between the steep foot-hills of Cnoc na Coinnich in Skye and Carn na Crimeanaich on the mainland, a narrow cleft of blue water - Kyle Rhea, the turbulent strait toward which wind and tide were urging us. As we approached the gap, our speed increased still more. The face of the sea changed, became streaked and lined with odd-looking ripples not born of the wind, and dimpled with sudden whirling eddies. It became more and more evident that the whole volume of water was in motion. One had the sensation of being about to shoot rapids. Over to starboard, by Glenelg Bay, the sea was breaking white in foaming overfalls. Faster still we went. The thrust of the tide became fiercer. Invisible hands seemed to be clutching and pulling at the keel. Gurglings and hissings filled the air. Suddenly a great glassy dome of green water, veined with white, boiled up from the depths right under our bows. The yacht slewed shorewards helplessly. The dome immediately became a whirlpool, and we yawed back again. Then the sea, like a river in spate, swept us into the Kyle. For two miles we slid between steep grassy hills, scarred by ravines, and then, almost before we could realize it, were shot out into the broader quieter waters of Loch Alsh, feeling somewhat as if we had come through a gorge'.

Our passage north was more majestic, holding to mid-channel under the long loops of the power cable that now feeds Skye from the mainland. The two huge pylons carrying the power lines stand on either side like the Fingalian giants who are said to haunt the banks of the narrows. A long curve westwards into Loch Alsh avoids the shoals on the eastern tip of Skye and leads directly towards the Kyle light. Leave the red buoy marking the String Rock to port, and the water in mid-channel is clear. The ruin set on the hill overlooking Kyleakin is Castle Moil, said to have been built by the daughter of a Norse king who was married to a MacDonald and known locally as Saucy Mary. Legend has it that she levied a toll from ships passing through the straits. What is more certain is that Kyleakin derives from the Norse, the 'akin' coming from King Haakon.

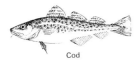

Cod

Kyleakin Narrows from the north

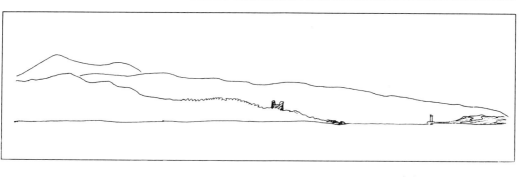

Kyleakin Narrows

Never have a pre-conceived idea about a stretch of coastline; always check the chart and Pilot. I offer that piece of advice without hesitation to all grandmothers, even those with a long experience of sucking eggs, because of what happened on passage to Plockton. *Hebe* was off Drumbuie in Loch Carron, sails pulling well in a good breeze and making her best possible speed. I pointed out the village to Trevor: 'That's where I spent weeks at a public inquiry into a plan to build huge concrete oil production platforms. The water, you see, is so incredibly deep here it was the only ...' I got no further than that. There was a horrifying crash as *Hebe* clattered against something extremely solid. Trevor looked over the side into this incredibly deep water and saw some jagged rocks jutting up close to the surface. *Hebe* had stopped but was still making some very unpleasant thudding sounds. The mast still stood, luckily, the hull was not holed so we took down the sails and eased her into deep water. It was then I read the Pilot: '... the southern shore of the entrance ... very foul ... the whole shore should be given a wide berth for 5 miles up', a warning amply confirmed by the chart which shows at half a glance a generous peppering of islets, rocks and shoal water along the entire south side of the loch. There could hardly be a worse place for negligent sailing, or for building 600 ft.-high oil platforms for that matter.

Plockton, a village with an oddly un-Scottish sounding name, nestles behind a headland and is one of the most delightful anchorages on the west coast. We were both shaken and demoralised by our experience off Drumbuie and were watching chart and position like a gannet looking for fish. There was the perch marking the Golach rocks and there the squat tower on Cat Island. We positioned all other hazards and watched a superb varnished sloop sail briskly past heading, by our calculations, directly for the Hawk Rock. Were we wrong again, were we about to go aground? Panic-striken, we did not return the cheery wave the group in the cockpit gave us as she swept by. We were too busy checking, prodding the bottom, poring over the chart. We heard the crash from several cables away. The mast shook like a baton conducting a pizzicato passage but she bounced off the Hawk undamaged. The cockpit became as active as a nest of ants. The skipper was examining his chart with his nose pressed against the paper. All was well. Two chastened crews entered Plockton that afternoon.

PLOCKTON

Map ref. 13F5
Water, (taps), hotels,
shops, PO

We anchored in perfect shelter from the south-west breeze off a stone pier at Ard Vour. Plockton anchorage itself has tropical trees, a colourful ribbon of houses along the shore and high mountains forming a backdrop. There is excellent holding ground although the tide retreats a long way from the shoreline. The village has stores, hotels and a number of public taps. There are rail connections to Inverness and even an airstrip.

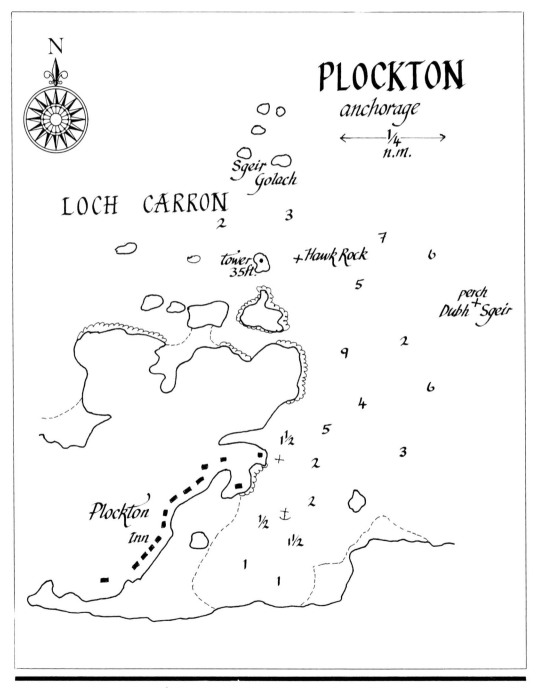

right Gometra North. A classically snug anchorage which opens from a narrow, steep-sided entrance
Fingal's Cave, Staffa, from within
over Sunset turns the sea of the Hebrides to gold

It was the second time I had tried to visit the Crowlin Islands at the elbow bend where the Inner Sound divides into Loch Carron and Loch Alsh. The first was on a wild day when a strong northerly gale howled directly down the narrow gut that splits the two islands as if they had been hit by an axe. A strong tide was flowing against the wind and the entrance was a mass of confused sea with a swell banging and foaming on the foul

CROWLINS

Map ref. 13E5
No facilities

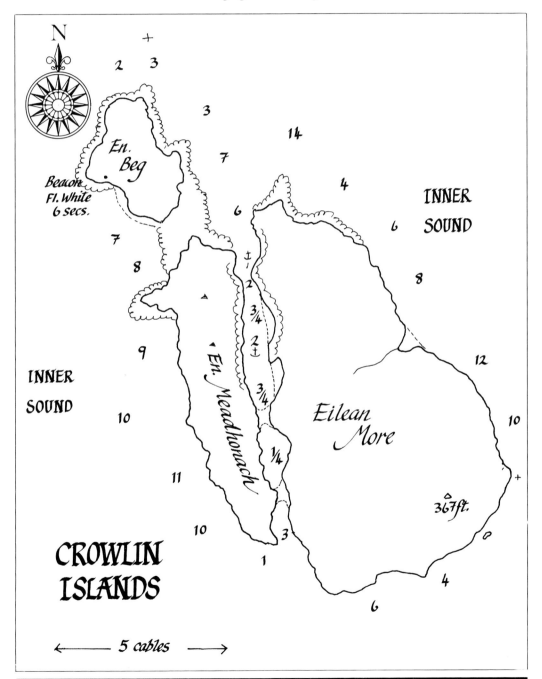

N

2   3

3

14

En.
Beg

3

7

Beacon
Fl. White
6 secs.

6

7

INNER

SOUND

6

8

7

8

En. Meadhonach

9

3/4

2
+

12

INNER

SOUND

3/4

Eilean
More

10

10

1/4

11

3

10

1

367ft.

CROWLIN
ISLANDS

4

6

←——— 5 cables ———→

left The anchorage behind Rubh-Ardalanish on the south coast of Mull gives near perfect protection in the loneliest surroundings
Sanna Bay lies behind protective reefs north of Ardnamurchan Point

ground around Eilean Beg. *Hebe* stood off, the wind rattling her headsail as we surveyed the unwelcoming entrance. The islands looked ominous, with bare slopes of drenched bracken and scrub and black, shattered cliffs gleaming wet. I let the sails fill and eased the boat onto a broad reach heading for the shelter of Toscaig Bay as rain was added to the gloom.

Crowlin Isles

On the second visit the islands were hardly recognisable as the same place. This time we had come up through Kyle with a spring tide and following wind in *Dorran*. The Crowlins were bathed in late afternoon sunlight, the air was warm and as the yacht ghosted through the shelter towards the first narrows, water green as bottle glass curved from the bows. The ominous island had become a place of subtle colour, and the weathered rocks were now grey and warm and decorated with bright patches of lichen. We anchored just short of the first narrows and went ashore. In *Hebe* I would have ventured further into the narrows. There appeared to be plenty of water, even where chart 2209 says there should be none, but *Dorran* was a fin keeler of much deeper draught. The responsibility of a bigger boat concentrates the mind.

POLL DOIN

Map ref. 13E5
No facilities

Hebe was swept into Poll Doin by a sudden hooligan squall that caught me with full sail up and wishing earnestly to escape into somewhere sheltered. It was a fortunate and very welcome bolt hole. I sorted out the tangle of sheets that developed when the squall pounced and *Hebe* suddenly luffed up. It was obviously the tail sting of a sudden gale that had heaped up the sea in long, black combers with breaking tops that were whipped off and left, in long streaks of foam, markers to the wind's path. They were suddenly not conditions for a small boat to be in. I headed up, got the main down and ran with the genoa only. The perch marking the outlying rock off Ard Bane flashed past and I eased *Hebe* round, gybing the genoa and preparing to start the engine or get the main up again if she started making leeway towards the Ruag rocks. Across the wind she behaved impeccably under headsail alone and I was able to shoot her into sheltered water at the head of Poll Doin. Down went the anchor and I watched above the trees as the clouds tore across the sky. Even in northerly winds this is a sheltered anchorage but with a south-westerly gale it was perfect and I celebrated an efficient deliverance with a large medicinal nip.

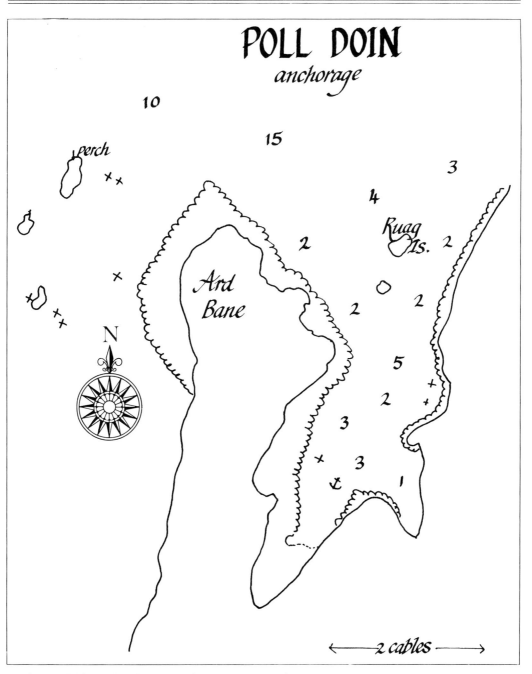

POLL DOIN
anchorage

10

15

perch

3

4

2

Ruag Is. 2

Ard
Bane

2

2

N

5

2

3

2

3

←——— 2 cables ———→

The wind blew all night but as the tide ebbed, *Hebe* sank even more snugly into her anchorage so that the only indication that there were strong winds around was a rustling sound in a fringe of rowan and hawthorn trees on the cliff top nearby.

There are some excellent walks from Poll Doin and on a fine day the beach that shows clearly on the west shore of Ard Bane is worth a visit. It is a perfect cove of pure coral.

PORTREE

Map ref. 13C5
All facilities
available

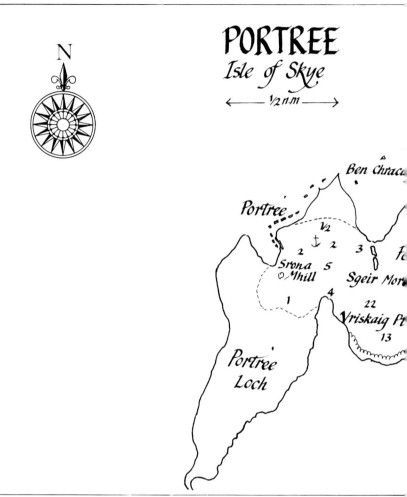

Herring Gull. Commonest gull on the coast; it breeds on cliffs, dunes, shingle, and bogs

Portree offers the closest approach to real fleshpots north of Oban. It is an excellent sheltered anchorage although after a month or more among the remote corners of the West, the noise of traffic and the glitter of street lights reflecting brightly on the water were curiously distracting. As the Pilot warned, we found the winds near An Tom point wildly confused, slapping the sails first one side then the other and throwing the boom around so much that I eventually took all the sails down and motored in past the long spit that runs out from the north side of the entrance and into the bay. There is fuel, a selection of hotels and all stores ashore. I even managed to track down a couple of bottles of Bull's Blood, one of which promptly disappeared in partnership with a pound or more of fine steak. Fleshpots are fine after a diet of powdered milk and meatballs in aspic.

We were four days in Portree living like a pair of kings whilst the wind howled down the whole west coast. Every day more yachts were blown in, most of them heavily reefed and those that were not burying their lee gunnels and making as much windage as a nun's chorus on stilts, as one sailing commentator described it.

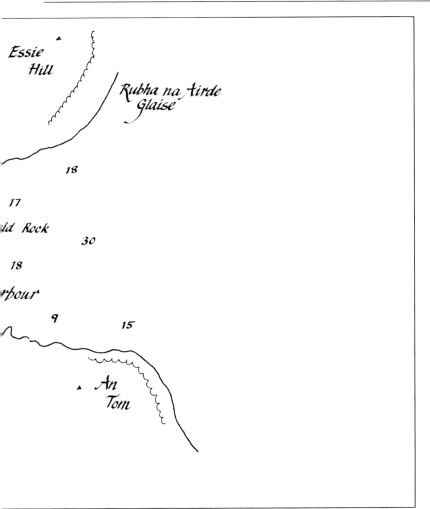

Essie Hill

Rubha na Airde Glaise

18

17

ld Rock

30

18

rbour

9

15

▲ *An Tom*

Portree, Isle of Skye

SOUTH RONA

Map ref. 12D4
Water (spring by path)

It is almost dark on this lonely hill above Acarsaid Mor. The last faint touches of green and grey are fading from the sky and Raasay has become a shadowy line with no sign of a light. Night and autumn are drawing close; you can feel it as a sharpness in the air that turns breath to vapour and gives an extra brilliance to the first stars. There is one other yacht in here but no other sign of life on the Skye shore and we have anchored close together for comfort perhaps. In the last light and the darkness before the moon rises I can pick out *Hebe's* white hull lying still in a black pool. No wind stirs the surface and an old building below me stands sinisterly dark.

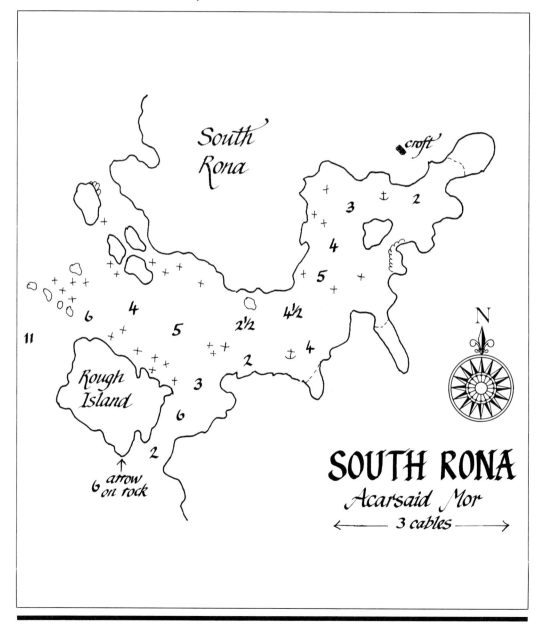

South
Rona

croft

3   2

4

5

4½

11   6   4   5   2½   2

Rough
Island   3

6

2

arrow
6 on rock

N

SOUTH RONA
Acarsaid Mor
←—— 3 cables ——→

Acarsaid Mor, South Rona

What a contrast with the afternoon, approaching the island from Portree, *Hebe* goose-winged to a fine breeze with all sails set and scampering across a sea bright with sunlight. I kept the wind astern so that the broken coastline of North Raasay slowly closed and in less than two hours' sailing I was cooking lunch in Fladday harbour. Another couple of hours with the breeze at no more than Force 2, *Hebe* drifted up to the large arrow mark on Rough Island and followed it into this perfect anchorage. The channel is clear except for one rock (see chart). The tide was high and I could see no sign of this lurking danger. I took down the sails and motored on towards the solitary house beyond the island at the head of the inlet. Ashore there was nothing but steep heather and rock hills that give perfect shelter. At one time Acarsaid Mor (Big Harbour) was an operational centre for smugglers and one early account described the fleet of 'thieves, ruggairs and reivairs' that sheltered there.

There are faint traces of the community that lived here before retreating to easier ground in the south of Raasay. Even for those hardy folk life on South Rona was tough. Water was scarce and in dry seasons had to be carried in from Skye. Four islanders returning once with fresh supplies foundered in the dark and wind after missing the elusive harbour entrance, and were all drowned.

Now there is only a drenched carpet of long, tough grass and rock covering Rona, the crumbled ruins of the old community's homes, and a few mysterious black boxes perched on the summits of the island belonging to the Ministry of Defence and used to monitor submarine exercises in the Inner Sound.

LOCH SHIELDAIG

Map ref. 12F4

Sailing off the west coast at night may be nerve-racking inshore unless conditions are clear, the navigator is absolutely certain of his position and he knows the waters well. Lights are sparse and aimed at assisting vessels on passage rather than guiding small cruisers into snug nooks on pitch dark nights. *Dorran* was 3 miles south of the wide mouth to Loch Torridon at dusk. The lighthouse on the tip of South Rona was sending regular paths of reflected brightness across the Inner Sound on the port bow. The bulk of the island stood ink black against the sunset. A faint katabatic breeze came from a shoreline barely visible to starboard. With the light bearing 270 degrees on the compass *Dorran* eased round the invisible bulk of Rudha na Fearn and onto a course that would clear the Trian rock. We were heading obliquely across the mouth of the loch until the loom of the northen shore appeared. Round onto a south-east course under power now, sails limp, and purring into black, star-covered space. The navigation lights seemed brilliant in that darkness. Holding to deep soundings on the depth gauge, *Dorran* cleared the solid bulk of Ru Ardheslaig and its outlying rocks and the night was suddenly punctured by a row of a dozen orange lights on the main street of the village. The bright glow showed the outline of Shieldaig Island and we headed for the second lamp on the left to clear the north end of the island which is shoal. The anchor went down in 2 fathoms in the curve of the bay, well clear of a rocky spit that runs from the shore to the southern tip of the island.

It is from Loch Torridon that the west coast opens out to the full send of the Minch and a stout boat is a necessity. Without the shelter of inner islands the waters are a serious challenge to a small craft and in the time that *Dorran*, a 34-ft. Rival, cruised north of Torridon we were able to put to sea in conditions that would have kept *Hebe* harbour-bound or facing a number of long and very uncomfortable passages. There is nothing to beat the solid muscle of a long keel and an inboard diesel when the barometer falls and the wind swings directly from the course you have to make.

BADACHRO

Map ref. 12E2
Water, inn, shop, PO

The day defied all the forecasts. Rain and strong northerly winds with poor visibility was the gloomy view from the meteorological experts for the sea area Hebrides. 'Got his isobars tangled, obviously,' the crew remarked, baring a pale chest to the hot sun. The genoa was full with a westerly wind and *Dorran* headed towards the entrance to Loch Gairloch, little more than a cable from the shore. The turn eastwards was made gradually around Sron na Carra until the bulge of Eilean Horrisdale appeared 1½ miles ahead. Standing in past its western end, we entered a land-locked harbour, small but clearly popular to judge from the number of moorings dotted around. We put the anchor down in 5 fathoms near a perch and went by dinghy to explore Horrisdale island with its row of old crofts, some of which have been finely restored as retreats or holiday homes; a sad reverse from the time the island boasted a community and even a pub.

The wide mouth of Loch Gairloch is open to anything the Minch cares to throw into it but Badachro receives little of the send from even the

Badachro and Horrisdale Island

strongest westerly. The village of Badachro has a Post Office, general grocery and a pub that offers food and baths.

Loch Shieldaig at the head of Loch Gairloch also gives good shelter. The loch branches off to the south and is entered easily by holding to the eastern shore away from the two islands. Nearby is Flowerdale House, with its own mud-bottomed bay. The building dates back to 1738 when the second baronet of Gairloch named the handsome house after the profusion of flowers in the district. It may not be obvious to anyone who actually dives into the sea, but the Gulf Stream flows this way.

Behind Inverewe Gardens

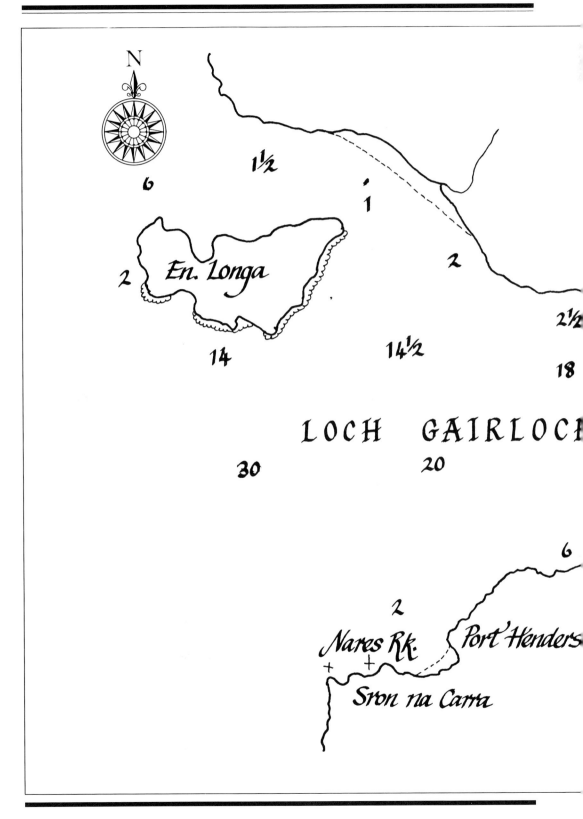

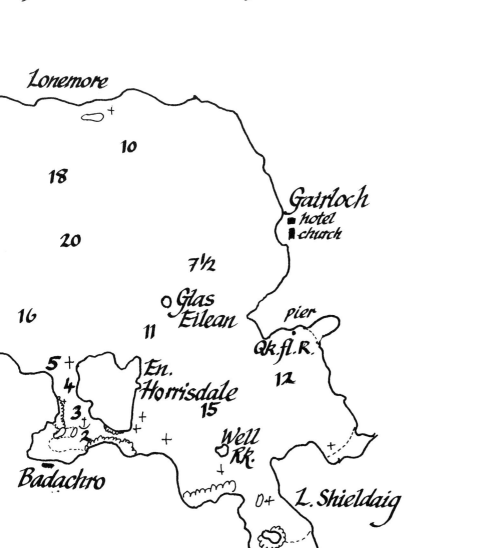

LOCH GAIRLOCH
Badachro Anchorage

←———— 1 ————→
n.m.

▲354ft. ▲535ft.

Lonemore

10

18

20

16

Gairloch
■ hotel
▮ church

7½

o Glas
Eilean

11

pier
• Qk.fl.R.

5 +
4
3
0 2

En.
Horrisdale
15

12

Well
Rk.

Badachro

0+ L. Shieldaig

Dipper. Breeds under tree roots and bridges near rivers; feeds on river bottoms, turning over pebbles in search of insects

4

Leac Bhuidhe
3 Mhor

2

N

2

2½

3

Leac Bhuidhe Bheag

1½

2

2½

Creagan na
Cudaigean

2

2

2

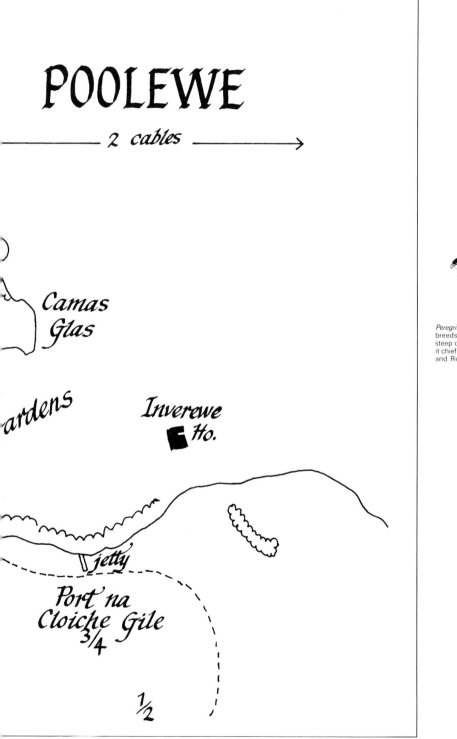

POOLEWE

⟶ 2 cables ⟶

Camas
Glas

ardens

Inverewe
Ho.

jetty

Port na
Cloiche Gile
¾

½

Peregrine. Large falcon which breeds on sea-cliffs and steep crags; a rare predator, it chiefly hunts Woodpigeon and Red Grouse

INVEREWE

Map ref. 12F2
Poolewe and Aultbea:
water, hotels, shops, PO

Summer Isles

Dab

Like an old grey cat waiting for the mice to appear, the fishery protection vessel *Vigilant* lay in the shelter of Longa Island with a faint wisp of warmth drifting from her smokestack. This is a favourite spot for the watchful vessels, with the whole of the Minch ahead. It accounts for the frequent appearance of Rubha Reidh, the headland to the north, as a point in cases of illegal fishing. The service, operated as a truly civilian navy by the Department of Agriculture and Fisheries for Scotland, has recently been brought up to date by the introduction of newer vessels, 35-knot patrol boats, and aerial survey flights to monitor the inshore fishing activity. The change from benevolent protector to keen gamekeeper has happened rapidly as a result of the threat to diminishing mackerel and herring stocks off the west coast from powerful purse seiners able to catch their week's quota, worth perhaps £20,000, in a matter of hours. The temptation to carry on earning, particularly when overhead costs run so high, is formidable. Hence the vigilance of *Vigilant*, tucked behind Longa, as we passed her close-hauled on port. Once more it was a sparkling mor-

ning and when we left the protection of the loch and caught the free wind, *Dorran* was trying to plane across the gentle swell. A brisk jibe around Rubha Reidh and half an hour's busy reaching eastwards brought us close to the mouth of Loch Ewe where the Minch swell swilled across some flat-topped rocks. Inside the loch the wind died and we started the engine. It was difficult to pick out the only obstacle, Sgeir an Araig, because in the flat evening light the substantial rock merged into the gold-brown colours of the Isle of Ewe. We kept in deep water and slipped into a quiet bay close to the jetty near the back gate to Inverewe gardens, which are one of the gems of the West Highlands.

It was one Osgood Mackenzie who began work in 1862 on transforming a barren headland, Am Ploc Ard, into a remarkable tropical garden. Soil was carried in creels to the high red sandstone mound to provide bedding for the plants. The wind that roared in from Labrador had stripped the land except for a solitary bush of dwarf willow, but Mackenzie saw the potential of the place under the benign influence of the ubiquitous Gulf Stream that flowed directly into the loch. A thick belt of Corsican pine and Scots fir was planted as a barricade against the scouring winds and salt spray and slowly, over the years, the gardens matured into a splendid legacy for the nation. Mackenzie's work was continued by his daughter, Mrs. Mairi T. Sawyer, who handed the gardens to the National Trust for Scotland in 1952, just before her death. Inverewe, in spite of its remote position, is one of the most popular attractions owned by the Trust. The variety of heaths, heathers, shrubs, trees and plants from all corners of the world is staggering and beautifully landscaped.

The fine spell ended as all fine spells must on the west coast. The sky was covered with a grey pall and drizzle came sniping in on the edge of a cold north-westerly. We motored *Dorran* into the shelter of Loch Thurnaig as a low from Shannon moved through with gale force winds, building up an unpleasant short sea on the loch outside. We had a meal in this quiet shelter and when the worst was over, the wind giving way to a steady downpour, *Dorran* headed up the loch on the eastern side of the Isle of Ewe which would also have given excellent shelter. A feature of Loch Ewe is the large number of buoys dotted about that make night navigation difficult. Today in the increasingly gloomy visibility, we headed out past the dark hull of a moored submarine. A watchman on the conning tower waved glumly as we passed and the sinister shape was slowly swallowed in the murk. The wind had backed and as *Dorran* cleared the loch we could feel the build-up of the sea towards Greenstone Point. Plugging both tide and wind we set a compass course for the Summer Isles which lay invisible behind the curtain of rain.

THE SUMMER ISLES

Map ref. 15A6
Water (well on Tanera More)

A long swell off the Summer Isles (John Cleare)

It was an uncomfortable sail into a heavy, confused sea. Priest Island emerged where it was expected on the port bow and as the wind died visibility improved. The cold, grey shapes of the Summer Isles - what an inappropriate name that day - loomed from the mist, then the mainland appeared with Ben More Coigach lifting a pencil line of a ridge steeply towards an invisible summit. The rocks jutting from the sea to the south

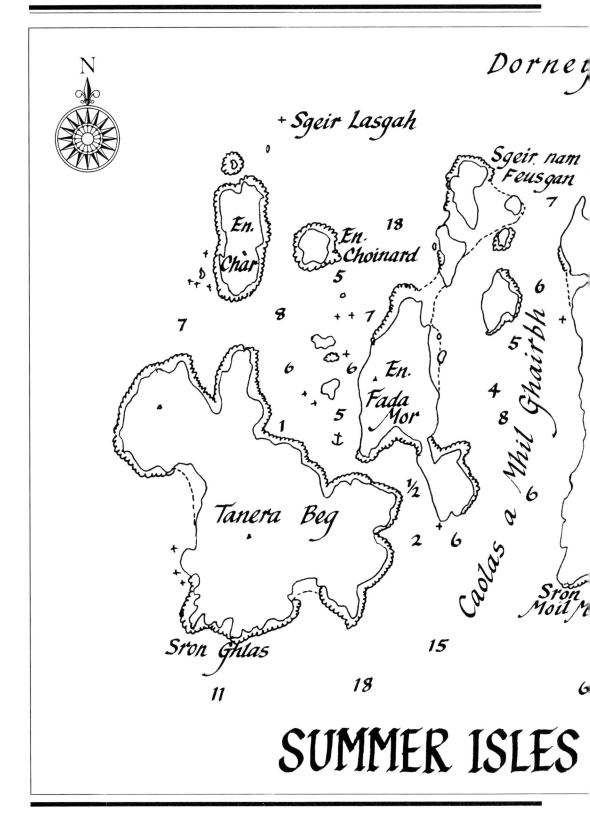

N

Dorney

+ Sgeir Lasgah

Sgeir nam
Feusgan

7

En.
Chàr

En.
Choinard

18

5

7

0

8

+ + 7

6

En.
Fada
Mor

Sgeir nam
Feusgan

5

6

4

8

6

7

6

6

5

5

1

5

⚓

½

Tanera Beg

2 + 6

Caolas a Mhil Ghairbh

Sron
Moil M

Sron Ghlas

15

11

18

6

SUMMER ISLES

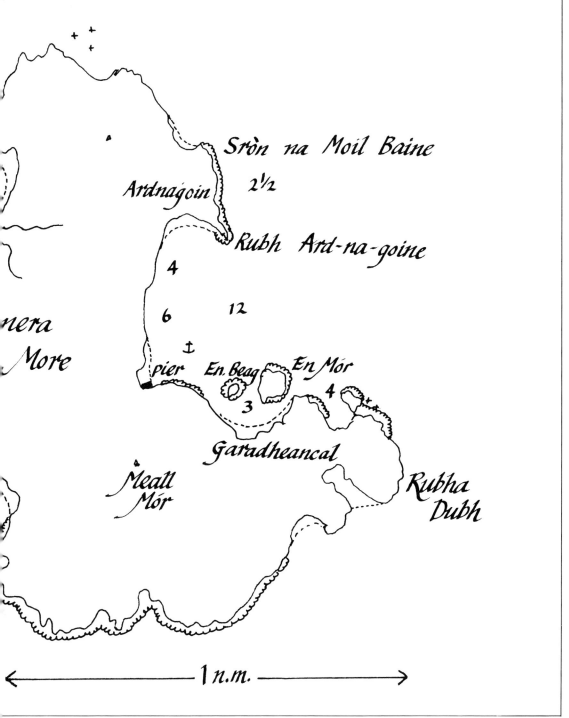

Sound

Sròn na Moil Baine

Ardnagoin

2½

Rubh Ard-na-goine

4

12

6

pier

En. Beag

En Mór

nera

More

3

4

Garadheancal

Meall Mór

Rubha Dubh

← 1 n.m. →

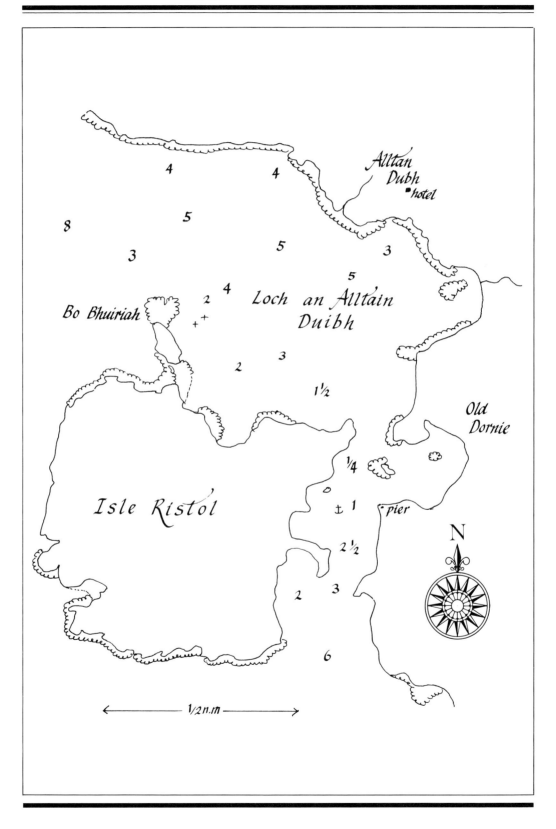

of Tanera More, the largest of the Summer Isles, looked particularly hostile. The wind died altogether and the rain beat the sea into a surface of dark pewter as we headed into the long channel dividing Tanera More and Tanera Beg. The water trickled down oilskins, gathered in pools in every fold and infiltrated every crack between skin and clothing. We steered a course into Dorney Sound well clear of the two hidden dangers in this area, Iolla a Mealan off the north mainland shore and Iolla Capall close to the main island.

Dorran motored quietly into the splendid open bay on Tanera More. There is good holding both near the pier and behind the small island known as the Cabbage Patch. This was one of John McLintock's favourite anchorages. He was here on a rougher day and recalled foaming across the bay on the tail-end of a hard squall that flicked across Baden Bay. 'The sun had set, but the high feathery lines of wind-blown cirrus still burned a rosy red against the deepening blue. Dark purple shadows draped the distant heights of Ben More Coigach, and across Baden Bay shone the cottage lights of Achiltibuie. We had doubled a few large corners in the search for romance that day, and now, beyond a doubt, we had it. Then, having stowed away and snugged down on deck, we went below, and, turning with Cape-Wrathful appetites to a gargantuan supper, neglected romance for materialism. Later, the yellow moon sailed over the eastward hills and stencilled a track of lambent fire on quiet waters. The wind had gone to a whisper; ripples grumbled somnolently on the beach; but if one listened, one heard a low, interminable undertone of sound - the voice of long seas still rolling past outside'.

Curlew. Insectivorous bird which breeds on grassy moors and peat-bogs; winters in marshy fields

Tanera More was once intended to be the centre of a thriving herring fishery and with Ristol and Isle Martin had curing stations in the late 1700s associated with the newly created fishing centre of Ullapool in Loch Broom. Huge shoals of herring swam around the Minch, keeping prosperous a large fleet of drift netters. In the 1820s the fish mysteriously disappeared and the curing industry died. The relics can be seen on Tanera More, the island where Dr. Fraser Darling, the naturalist, lived for some time.

In recent years fishing has revived spectacularly in Loch Broom when the East European 'Klondikers' arrive to take on the mackerel shoals caught by purse-seiners, mainly from the east coast. More than 30 factory ships from Russia, Bulgaria and East Germany anchor in Annat Bay or the upper reaches of Loch Broom and send a whiff of true fishing industry over Ullapool, returning the port to its original purpose. Indeed 'Klondike' means not only profiting from a rich source of wealth but also the export of fresh herring direct from Scotland to the continent.

A sudden grey rain-squall came hissing out of the north-west in the late evening. We decided that the fleshpots of Achiltibuie were irresistibly attractive in such filthy, unsettled weather, so *Dorran's* anchor was hauled on deck - no mean feat in such a wind and without a winch - and we headed at last light for the snug anchorage in a narrow-necked pool east of Ristol. That night the wind raged but *Dorran* hunted gently around her anchor cable, in the way of all Rival 34's, and we slept soundly.

LOCHINVER

Map ref. 15B5
Water, (taps), hotels,
shops, PO

On the torn, complex coastline of Enard Bay, Lochinver is not hard to position. The high sugar loaf shape of Suilven rises slightly to the south of the town, which is hidden at the head of the deep cut. The steep-sided isle of A'Chleit and the twin-topped island of Soyea also provide direction. It was a bright, clear morning when *Dorran* sailed downwind past Kirkaig Point and into the hidden reaches of the loch. Glas Leac was clear ahead 2 miles away. Several fishing boats low on the waterline overtook us on their way in to unload catches at the fishery quay. Lochinver has stores, pubs and an excellent chandlery if you are looking for shackles one foot across and fenders that would ward off a battleship. The Culag Hotel also provides a hot bath and a comfortable lounge where, pink and fragrant, the freshly-bathed sailor can recover from the bill - £2.50p at 1981 prices.

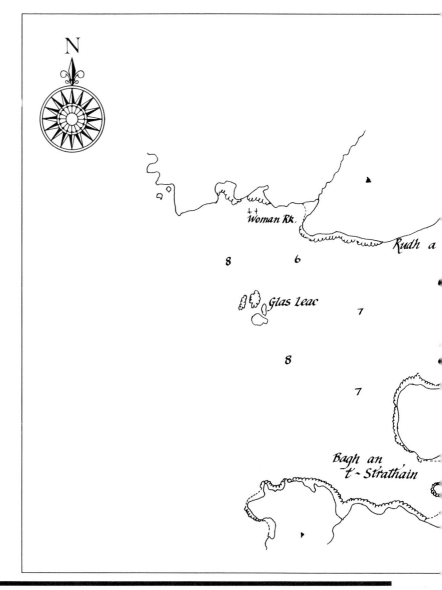

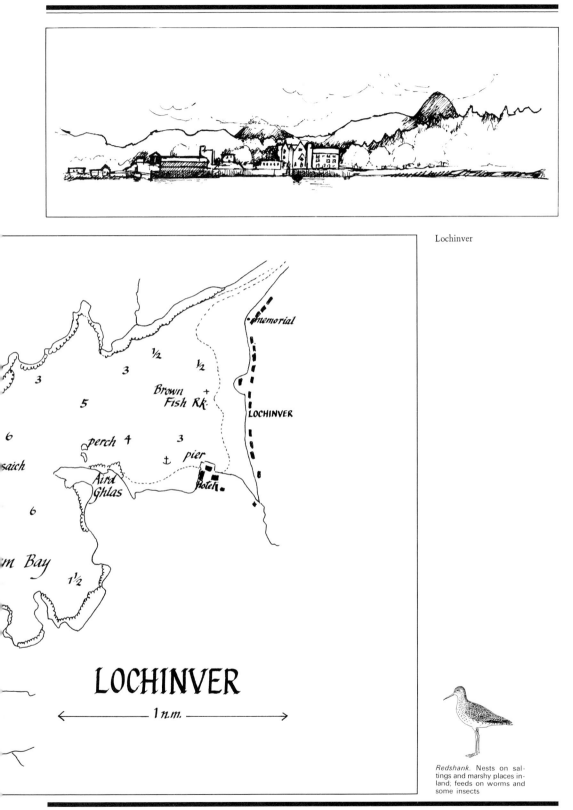

Lochinver

½

3

3

½

Brown
Fish Rk.

+

memorial

LOCHINVER

5

6

perch 4

3

saich

± pier

Aird
Ghlas

Hotel

6

n Bay

1½

LOCHINVER

← 1 n.m. →

Redshank. Nests on sal-
tings and marshy places inland; feeds on worms and
some insects

LOCH ROE AND LOCH NEDD

Map ref. 14B4
Drumbeg: water, inn, shop, PO

The morning sun streamed over Loch Inver as *Dorran* cruised in deep soundings off the coast of Sutherland. The optical illusion of the foreground fleeting past, whilst the huge old giants of the north-west, Quinag, Canisp, Ben More and Sail Ghorm, remained anchored firmly in the background, was striking. The coastline here has been described as the last true wilderness in Europe, a place without rural quaintness or any modern refinement; an emptiness filled with the sound and colour of the sea and hills, the wild din of black-backs and guillemots, razor bills and arctic terns and the eternal rhythm of the ocean.

One of the most secluded anchorages of the entire west coast lies an hour's fast sail from Lochinver around the beetling headland of Rudha Rodha. Loch Roe winds into the hills behind Cnoc na Moine, foiling the worst swell and the strongest wind. It would be unwise to try to enter in a westerly gale with a heavy sea running; the channel leaves no room for manoeuvre and is guarded by the Ondine Rocks, but once inside, Pool Bay gives the ideal shelter. There is a pair of cairns on the north shore pointing to the channel leading clear of the reef and a shallow bar before the deeper waters of the pool. We anchored and listened to the silence.

Outside, the wind had veered into the west and piped up to Force 5. We quickly had *Dorran's* main and genoa set and drawing lustily. The boat heeled 30 degrees, slicing the bow through the swell and sending back cascades of spray that lit miniature rainbows. Stoerhead jutted out on the bow and *Dorran* hardened up to give the rugged headland a good off-ing. The coast fell back to the Point of Stoer marking the southern extremity of Eddrachillis Bay. Wind and tide swept us along on a fast reach with *Dorran* revelling in the action. Astern the pinnacle of rock known as the Old Man of Stoer began really to resemble an old, hunched figure. As the boat held a steady course into the bay so the old man appeared slowly to be turning his head.

Stoerhead

Eddrachills
Bay

11

15

8

2½

2½

1½

Quinag

to Drumbeg

LOCH
NEDD

←——— 2 cables ———→

* no longer visible

Eddrachillis is a large triangle that funnels into Loch Cairnbahn but we were steering around the northern tip of Oldany Island searching for the entrance to Loch Nedd. The coast was dotted with outlying rocks against which the sea pounded into brilliant breakers. This was sailing quite at its best. The entrance is not easy to see because we were approaching oblique-ly, but by aiming to the right of the massive bulk of Quinag we came abeam of an obvious square-shaped rock. The woodland that cloaks the valley around the loch opened up. Down with the main as *Dorran* slipped into flat water under the strong pull of the genoa. The rush of water and the surge of the hull through the steep seas died away. The air was warm and filled with the song of land birds in this idyllic anchorage. The loch runs south for about ¾-mile. Near its head, where a headland juts out narrowing the loch to about 1 cable, is good shelter in any weather. Beware of tucking too far towards the southern end; there lies the wreck of the *Empress of Bermuda* which broke adrift under tow to the breakers' yard and came to rest in this remote lagoon. The remains of her hull now show only at low water springs. There is a small stone pier on the south-western shore and stores, a Post Office and a pub at Drumbeg village 1½ miles to the west.

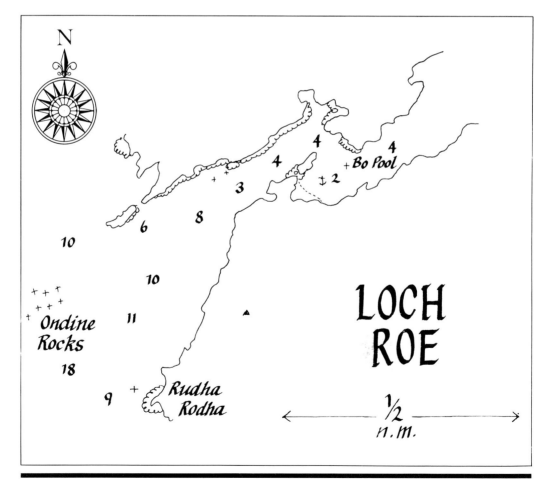

Loch Nedd

The hunched figure of the Old Man of Stoer

HANDA

Map ref. 14B3
Water (tap by RSPB
shelter)

Handa lies off the northern corner of Eddrachillis Bay, an island of birds. For 20 years it has been leased by the Royal Society for the Protection of Birds who manage the island on behalf of the 100,000 seabirds that inhabit the superb cliffs on the north-west shore and the 5,000 visitors that arrive in this remote spot each year from Britain and abroad. It is roughly 1½ miles by 1 mile, an island virtually abandoned by humans but superbly rich in bird life. Martin Allison, resident warden and an ecologist from Cumbria, met us on the fine sand beach by the anchorage at Port an Eilein. It was a fine evening and we set out immediately across the island. We walked along duckboards made by RSPB work parties out of drift-wood to protect the fragile machair from 5,000 pairs of tramping feet.

Until the mid-nineteenth century more than 100 families lived on Handa. The ruined remains of their cottages and the clear imprint of their lazy-bed cultivation can still be seen. It was a self-sufficent society that lived on a staple diet of oats, potatoes, fish and - like their contemporaries on St. Kilda - sea birds. Also in common with the St. Kildans, the Handa folk had their own queen and parliament.

In 1847 there was a potato famine on the island and the following year the laird of Handa decided to turn the 766 acres of the island into an extensive sheep walk. The two blows led to the clearance of the island and the folk of Handa sailed off to the New World.

For a place with so many birds, the island was remarkably silent. 'Sea birds don't sing,' Martin Allison said, 'but you can hear a snipe drumming over there and quite a few land birds get blown here in the easterly gales. They stay until the wind drops. We had a very surprised tree sparrow blown here like that recently ...' - (I did not see a single tree on Handa. Neither did the sparrow) -'... and a red throated pipit arrived with the gales from Scandinavia. When the strong winds blow from the west it brings gannets, manx shearwaters and storm petrels to Handa.'

Handa anchorage

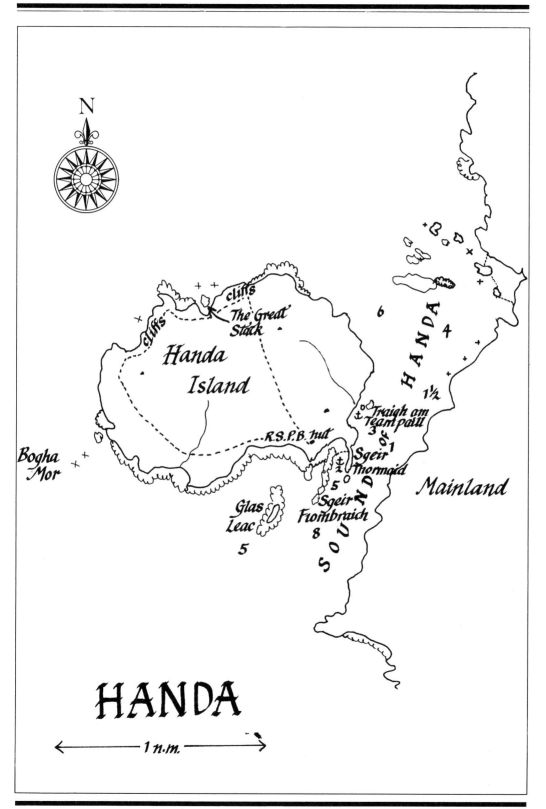

HANDA

← 1 n.m. →

It is the 400 ft. high cliffs of red Torridon sandstone that are the real attraction of the island and where the tens of thousands of seabirds are found. The Great Stack alone holds 12,000 birds with huge numbers of guillemots, kittiwakes and razorbills. In the grass on the summit of the stack and quite unassailable there are puffin burrows. Various types of whale are seen in the sound between Handa and the mainland. Dolphins are quite common in July and August and the Atlantic grey seal can be seen in good numbers.

Handa ranks as one of the most fascinating small islands off the west coast and the pathway from Port an Eilein across the island to the cliffs and back along the west coast is superb. The entrance is clear from the south, heading for the flagpole past Glas Leac and the string of rocks known as Sgeir Fiombraich. The water is deep and the holding good well up towards the beach. A shelter with information about the reserve is set back from the beach and behind the hut is a tap.

Great Stack, Handa, a pillar of seabirds

The reddish rocks of Ardmore Point mark the entrance to Loch Laxford less than 3 miles north of Handa. This is a superb sailing area on its own with a maze of bays, cuts and islets to explore. The name comes from the Norse; 'lax' meaning salmon and 'ford' from fiord, and a notable salmon river flows into the loch from Loch Stack which also contains sea-trout and fine brown trout. Two peaks dominate the view inland; Ben Arkle (2580 ft.) has a broad, rounded summit with a whiteness that can suggest perpetual snow; Ben Stack (2364 ft.) to the south has a sharp, conical shape.

It was a rough sail into a cold north-westerly from Handa, keeping well clear of a string of islands to starboard. The loch runs south-east for about 3½ miles. The wind gusted and blustered, the cold rain poured down oilskins and we had to keep the hatch thoroughly battened. One mile into the loch from Ardmore we passed Paddy's Isle close to the shore. A channel 1 cable wide led into Loch a Chad Fi and in the prevailing wind, seeking good shelter, we turned into the inner loch close by the timber buildings of John Ridgway's adventure-outdoor sports school. John and his wife live in the house far above the school and watch the arrivals and their efforts closely. We eventually ended up sheltering from the northerly squalls in the pool to the east of the small island. We laid out an ample length of chain and *Dorran* lay back on the anchor which was well embedded in excellent holding ground. Some instinct brought the two of us on deck early the next morning; perhaps the rustle of kelp against the keel. The wind had swung through 180 degrees, *Dorran* was now rapidly approaching shoal water on a descending tide. We pulled ourselves clear in time to the surprise of John Ridgway and his students who were using us as an object lesson of the necessity to keep an anchor watch. More than 60 anchorages and they were still teaching us something. The West had not finished, though; the wind remained on the nose all the way back.

LOCH LAXFORD

Map ref. 14C3
No facilities

Loch a Chad Fi (Glyn Satterly)

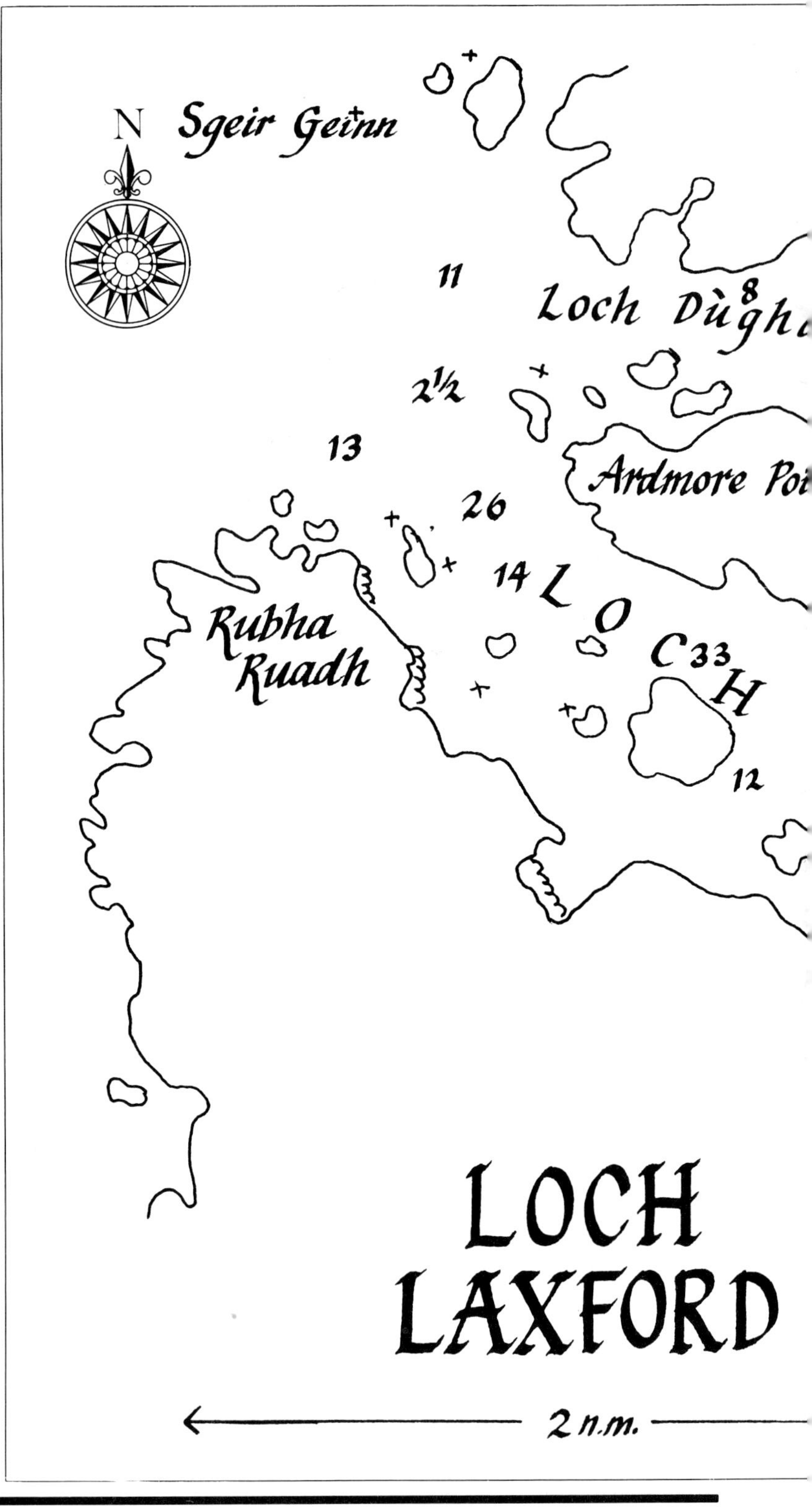

N

Sgeir Geinn

11

Loch Dùgh 8

2½

13

26

14 L O

Ardmore Po

C 33

Rubha
Ruadh

H

12

LOCH
LAXFORD

← ——————————— 2 n.m. ———

10

Portlevorchy

3½ *Loch a' Chau Fi*

7 +

+

Paddy's Is.

+

2

A +24 F O 10 R 7 D

+

7

+

5

5

1½ 4

½

Ringed Plover. Breeds on sandy and shingle beaches, or in gravel beds inland; outside breeding season it flocks on muddy and sandy shores. Feeds on molluscs, crustacea, insects

right The morn rises above *Dorran* in the anchorage at Handa, the island of birds
The quiet port of Poll Doin, the north-facing anchorage off the Inner Sound
over The old harbour at Craighouse, Jura. Only very shallow-draft craft can enter. The
alternative is the new pier to the east.

Sternpiece

A cold west wind blew with full hostility down Loch Carron and over the rooftops of Plockton. There was no disguising that the end of the season had arrived with lead-grey skies frowning on the local yachtsmen as they pulled their boats up high on the small beach of shingle just off the main street and secured them for the winter. *Hebe* had to be returned to Oban within days, a long haul for a small boat. Peter, a professional skipper, offered to help me sail her south. He explained that he wanted to test a new brand of sea-sickness pill that would perhaps revolutionise his working life.

We left in haste and the teeth of a south-westerly squall. *Hebe* was soon putting the pill through its paces, bouncing uncomfortably over a sealane of short, narrowly-spaced waves in Loch Carron. At least we caught the tide and slipped neatly through Kyleakin and on past anchorages and bays that earlier in the season we had plumbed and explored on our leisurely way north.

Time now pressed. In late autumn the wind had a sharp impatience about it. At the exit to Kyle Rhea, it blew against the strengthening tide causing a confusion of waves and back eddies. The boat bucked and swayed through the turbulence under engine. We took the sails down because the constant thrashing from side to side merely spilled the wind from them. Out in the Sound of Sleat the wind strengthened and slammed into the bows. Long tack followed long tack but the gain of distance was miserably small.

The darkness crawled upon us accompanied by rain squalls that quickly blotted out the lights of Mallaig and the Small Isles. Peter's watch was going none too well, what with the rain and the absence of a wheelhouse. He leaned into the cabin and began to thumb through the damp pile of charts. 'We are about to sail off the bottom of 2208 and I can't lay my hands on 2207. The wind's a good deal stronger and the visibility is appalling. Apart from that, I'm a bit worried about Ardnamurchan and the rocks west of Arisaig,' he declared gloomily.

left Across the Sound of Raasay from South Rona towards the Isle of Skye
The lighthouse on the south-east tip of Isle Ornsay early in the day

I buried myself deeper in my sleeping bag as the boat curtsied her way into the wind. We dare not use the engine now in case it was needed for a long spell to round Ardnamurchan. No chart, not enough fuel, the wind against us and the 'Cape Horn of the West' ahead of us, invisible in the worsening weather. Misery. I dug myself even deeper into the warm folds, listening to the wind rushing against the canvas and the thumps of Peter's boots above my head as he struggled to adjust the sails. At least the pill seemed to be working.

By the early hours, *Hebe* was still ploughing to and fro, by rough calculation somewhere south of Maxwell Bank. I handed Peter a hot drink as I came on watch. He was sitting shivering in the wet cockpit, the tiller in one hand and a road atlas in the other. Half a mile to port, a light was flashing, 'God knows what that is. They don't even have traffic lights on road atlases,' he said icily, the rain trickling off his oilskins.

A mildewed copy of Reed's Nautical Almanack was produced and after a damp scramble through its pages we identified the light as Bo Faskadale rock. Peter had succeeded in keeping a healthy westing well clear of Arisaig. He drew a course on the AA map and gave me a heading, then disappeared below.

Ardnamurchan still lay 7 miles ahead, further in fact because we would have to give the headland a wide offing to be safe. The next hour was cold, uncomfortable and frustrating. I cursed not having a bigger boat, a

Red Grouse. Only bird that is unique to Britain. It nests in heather and peat-bogs, but in winter leaves high ground; feeds on berries and insects

proper chart, even an improper chart, a diesel engine and the day that I even thought about sailing among these wet, hostile islands. I thought about people ashore comfortable and warm in their beds. Bo Faskadale blinked at me through the murk and cold rain soaked into my woollen hat. Even my hat was wrong. To add a trench to my low spirits I started to feel seasick for the first time that year.

The drizzle turned to rain and a steady wind began to belly the dripping sails. There was a positive whispering of water as *Hebe* began to surge forward. The mist thinned, the rain stopped and the breeze shifted obligingly several points starboard allowing *Hebe* to point due west. Magically the sky cleared and filled with stars. A near-full moon broke in bright splashes on the surface of the sea. Bravo for a classic clearing shower. Ardnamurchan lay like a black finger to port, the lighthouse still obscured by the nearest coast but its loom clear to see.

The Small Isles were dark, anchored shapes finely outlined against a frosty sky. Eigg flashed its position to me and soon Ardnamurchan Light was sending long blades of silver swathing across the waves. The veer in the wind allowed us to point well clear and *Hebe* raced along, sheets taut and sails full, across a huge pool of quicksilver. The misery was already forgotten. This was it, I told myself. This was sailing in The West. Now, what about next year . . .

The West

Practical Information

YACHT CHANDLERS

This list makes no claim to be inclusive

Edinburgh Area
Bosun's Locker, Port Edgar Marina, Shore Rd, South Queensferry
031-331-3875
Capital Yachts Ltd, 5 West Shore Rd, Edinburgh 031-552-8396
Seaspan, West Harbour Rd, Edinburgh 031-552-2224
Tulloch Boat Centre, 20 Canonmills Bridge, Edinburgh 031-556-7862

Glasgow Area
Angus Glass Co. Ltd, 56 Tannoch Drive, Lenziemill, Cumbernauld 31057
Duncan Yacht Chandlers, 7 Scotland St and 47 West Nile St, Glasgow
041-429-6044
Kelvin Hughes, 375 West George St, Glasgow 041-221-5425
Scotsail Equipment (Glasgow) Ltd, Woodholme Erskine, Ferry Rd,
Bishopton 216

Paisley
Giltron, Boatyard, Abercorn St, Paisley 041-887-2204

Greenock
William Turner and Son, 39 Arthur St, Greenock 21915

Oban
Nancy Black, 24 Argyll Sq, Oban 62550

Mallaig
John Henderson and Sons, Harbour Slipways, Mallaig 2304

Loch Carron
Ross Sailing Ltd, North Strome, Lochcarron 355

Ullapool
Highland Coastal Trading Co., Anchor Centre, Ullapool 2488

Tobermory
Seafare, Seafront, Tobermory 2277

Essential reading is the Clyde Cruising Club's *Sailing Directions* (10th edition, 1974, with five subsequent sets of amendments 1975-1981), available to non-members for £15, and £1 for each set of amendments. A list of publications and order form may be obtained from Clyde Cruising Club, S.V. *Carrick,* Clyde St, Glasgow Gl 4LN (041-552-2183).

The Scottish Tourist Board, 23 Ravelston Terrace, Edinburgh EH4 3EU (031-332-2433), publishes amongst its many useful booklets and guides *Adventure and Special Interest Holidays in Scotland,* which contains some information on sailing.

Admiralty charts and hydrographic publications are available from officially appointed agents, a full list of whom is obtainable from HMSO. The following selection will, it is hoped, be useful to the west coast sailor:-
Aultbea, Ross-shire: Bridgend Stores
Crinan, Argyll: Crinan Boats Ltd.
Edinburgh: Chattan Security Transport Ltd, 5 Canonmills
Glasgow: Kelvin Hughes, 375 West George St, G2 4LR
         Christie & Wilson, 44 York St, G2 8JW
Stornoway, Isle of Lewis: Duncan MacIver Ltd, 7 Maritime Buildings
Tarbert, Argyll: W.B. Leitch & Son

PUBLICATIONS

There are many firms engaged in bare boat and skippered chartering. The following selection consists of members of Associated Scottish Charters, Clynder, Dunbartonshire G84 OPZ:-
Arden, (Argyll) Ltd, Kilmelford, Oban 08522 248
North Channel Yachts, Stroul Bay, Clynder, Dunbartonshire 043683 430
Ross Sailing, Lochcarron, Ross-shire 05202 355
Seol Alba, Ardvasar, Isle of Skye 04714 262
Summer Isles Charters, Altnaharrie Inn, Ullapool, Wester Ross
                                                    085483 230

Skippered Charter
Fingal Yachts Ltd, Ardfern, by Lochgilphead, Argyll 08525 283
Gill Yacht Charters, Ardfern, by Lochgilphead, Argyll 0742 746029
Modern Charters, Shore Rd, Clynder, Dunbartonshire 043683 312

YACHT CHARTERING

Index

Map Section

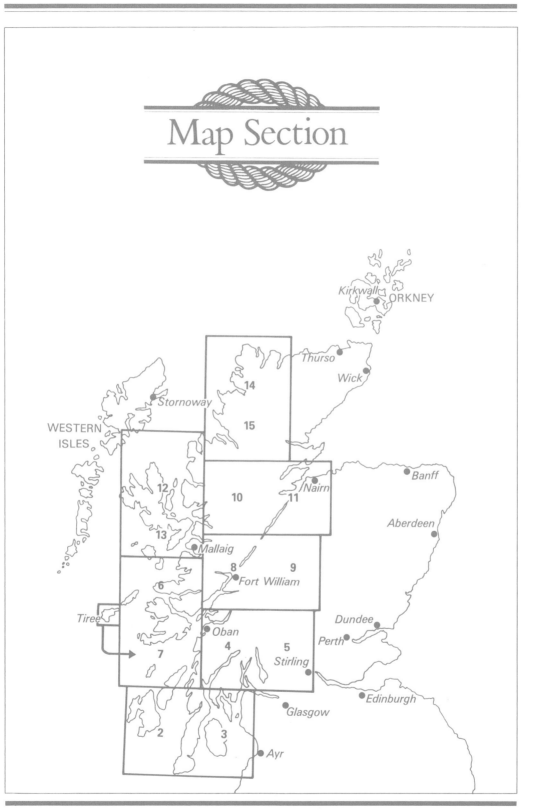

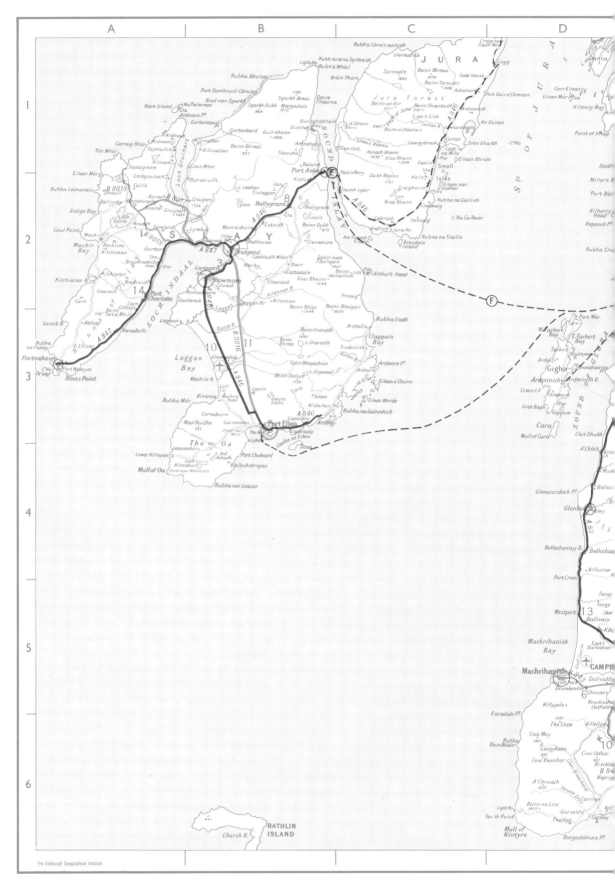

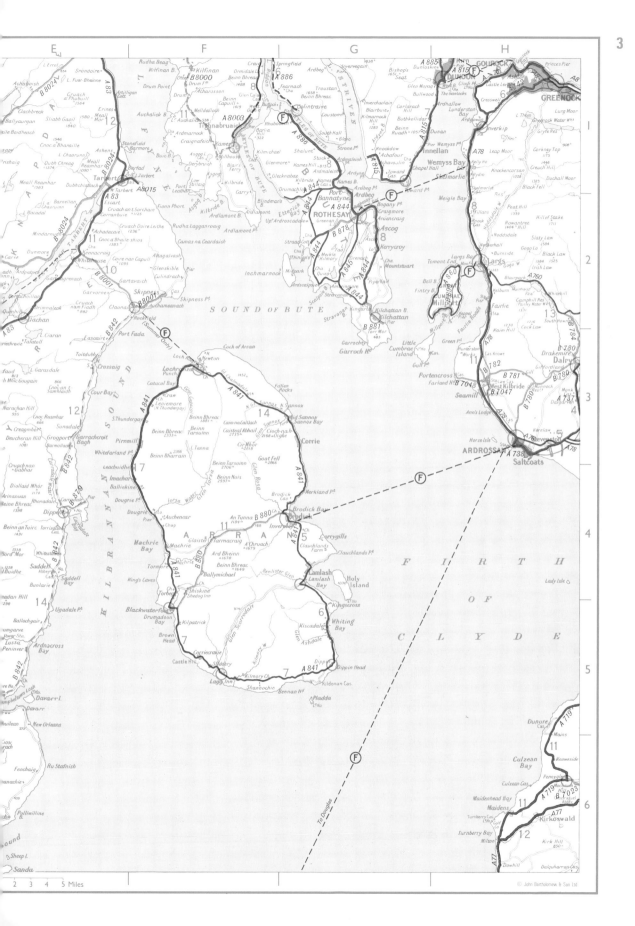

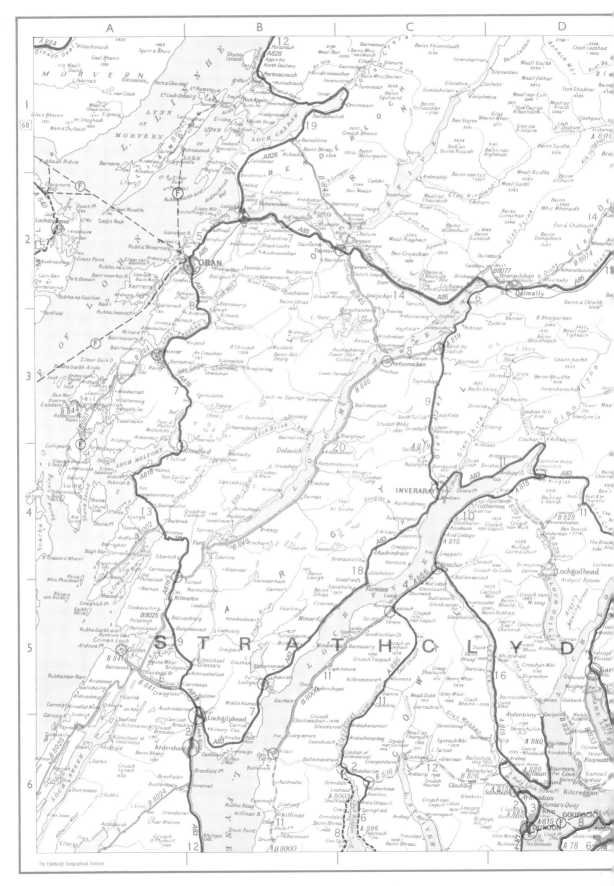

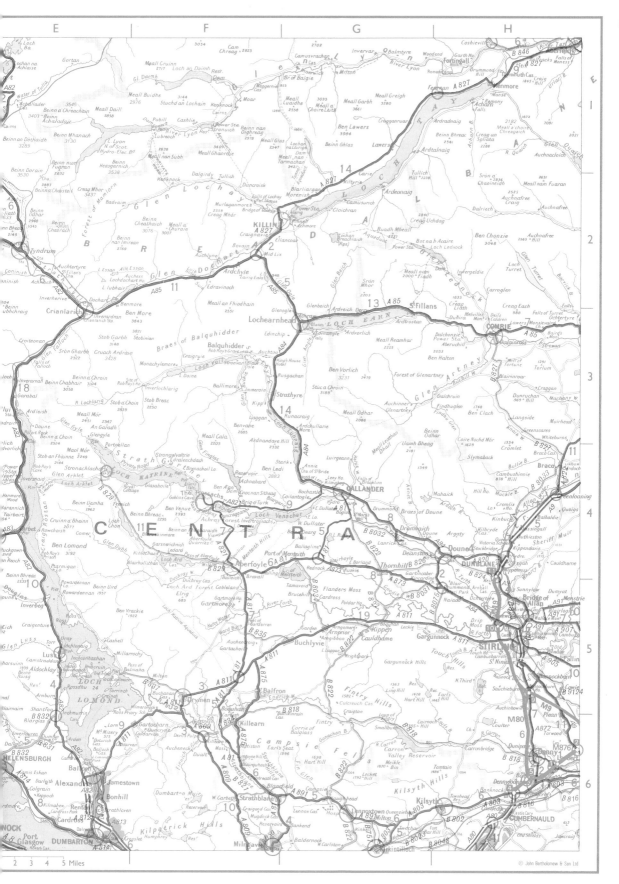

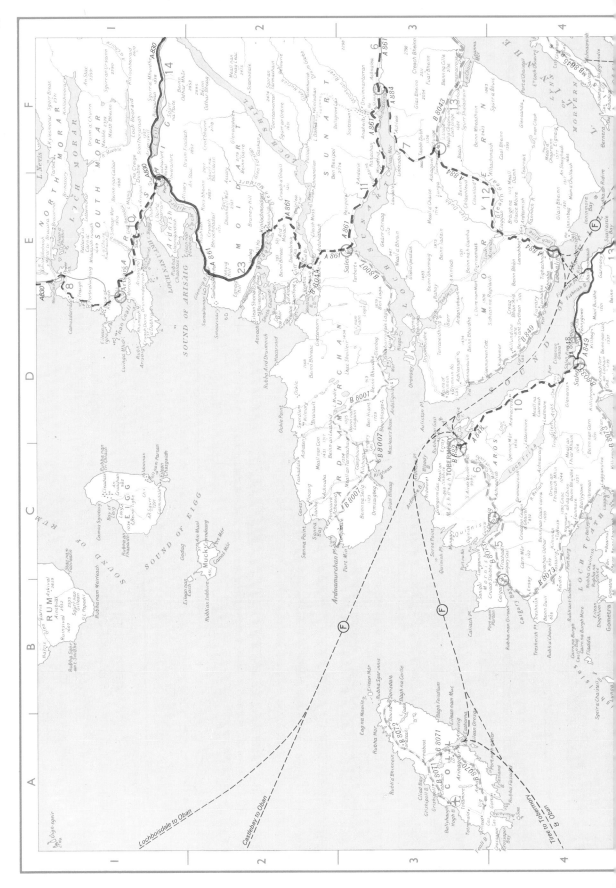

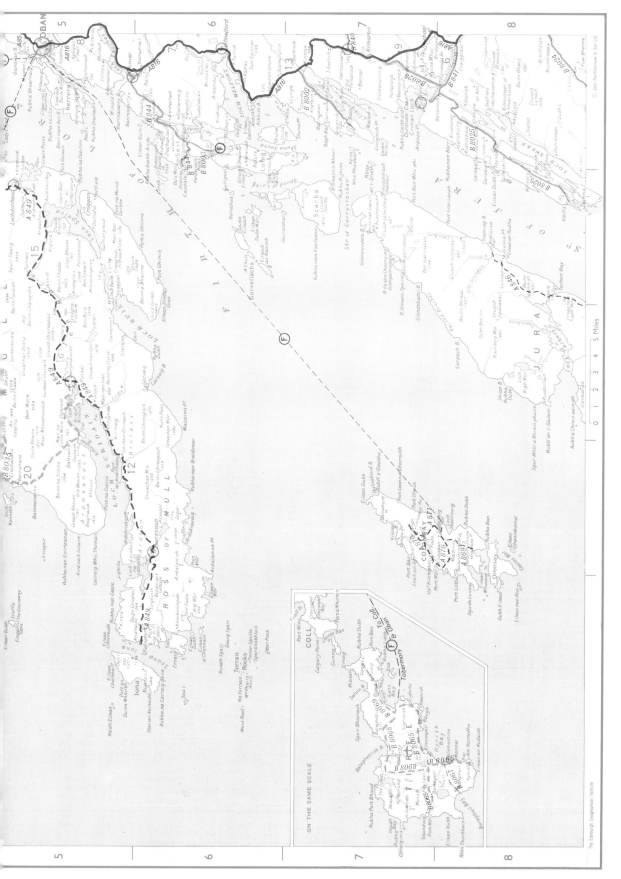

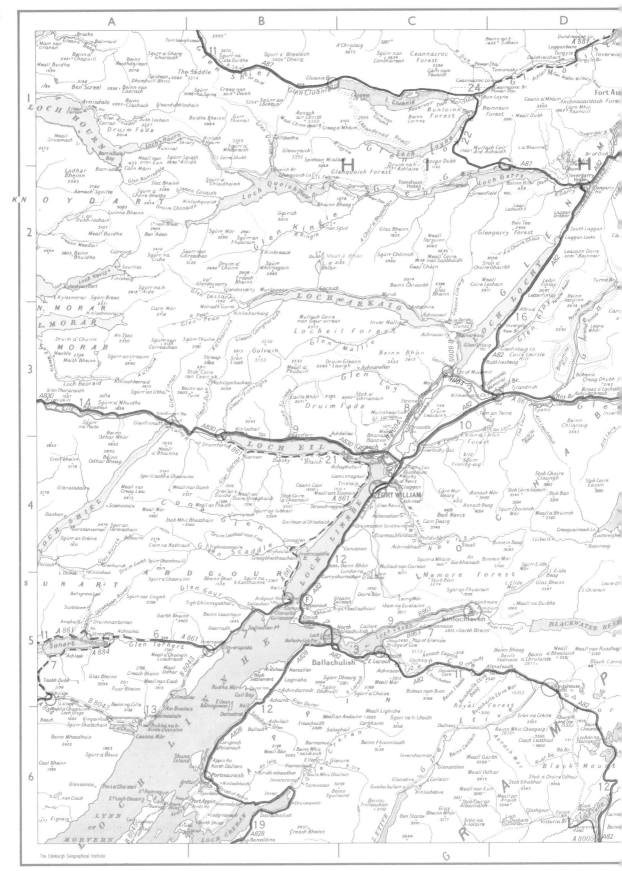

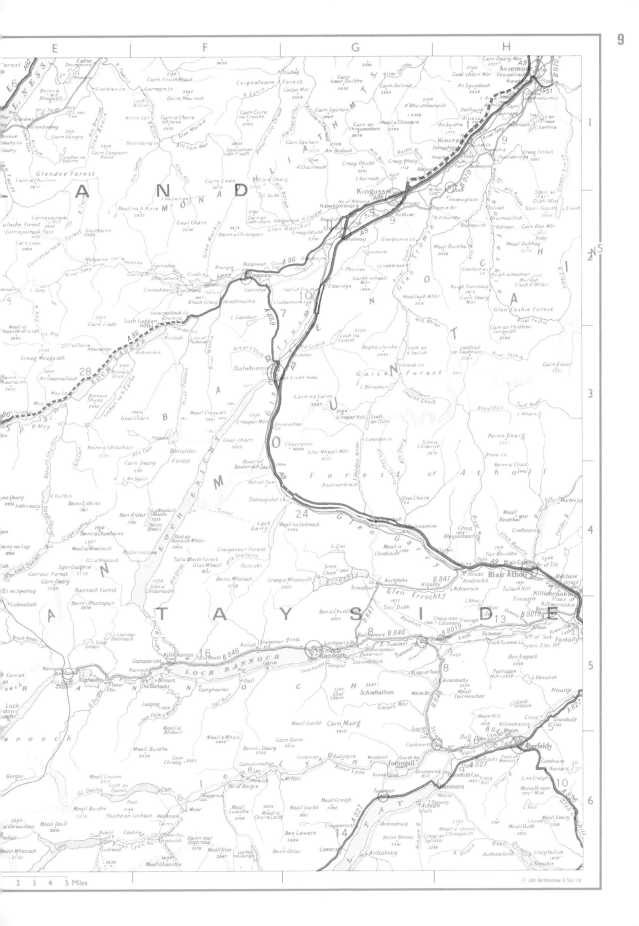

© John Bartholomew & Son Ltd

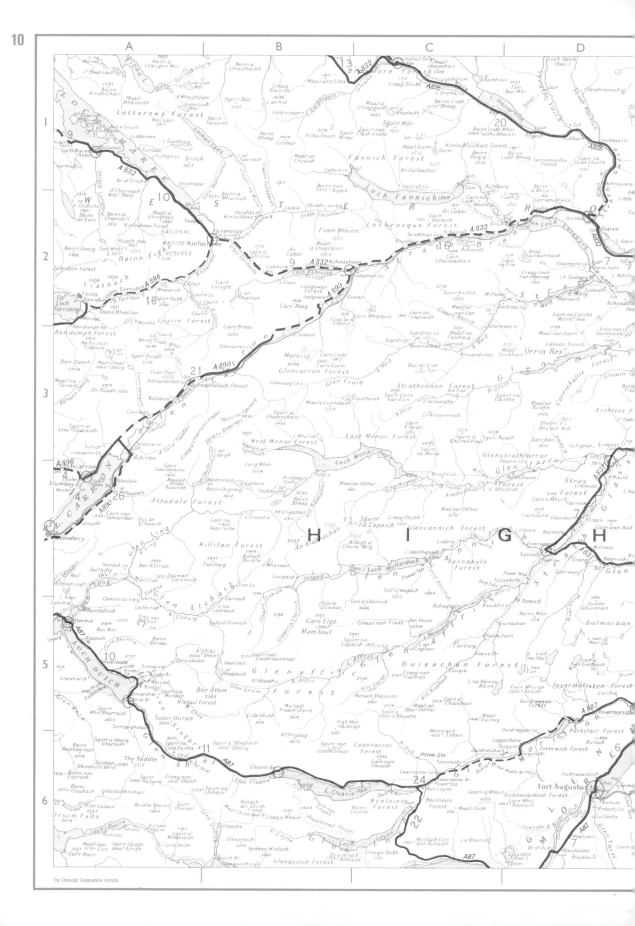

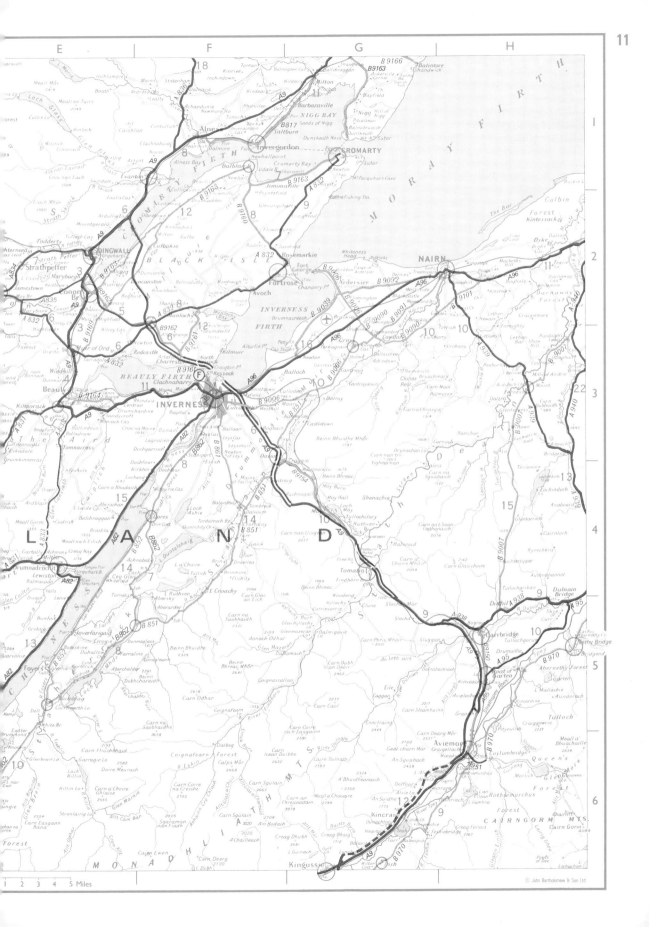

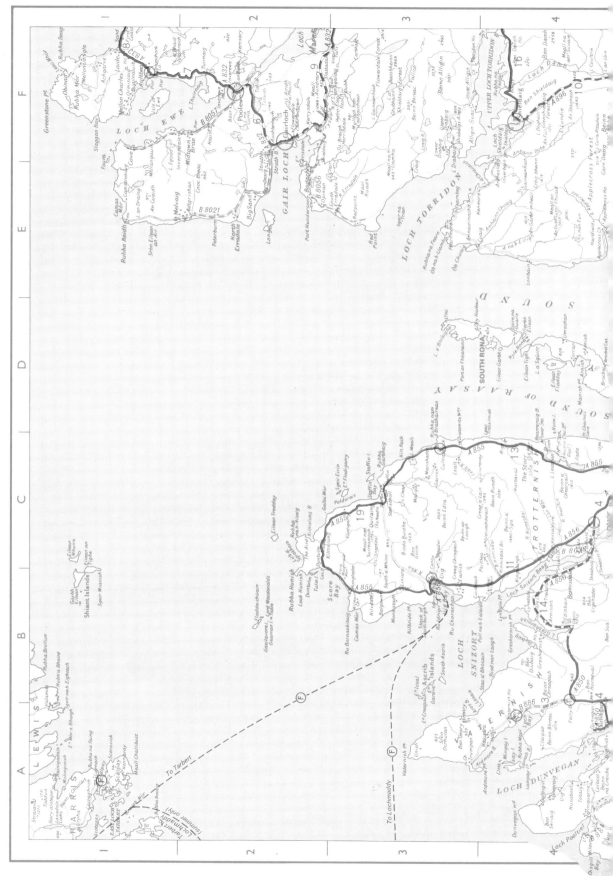

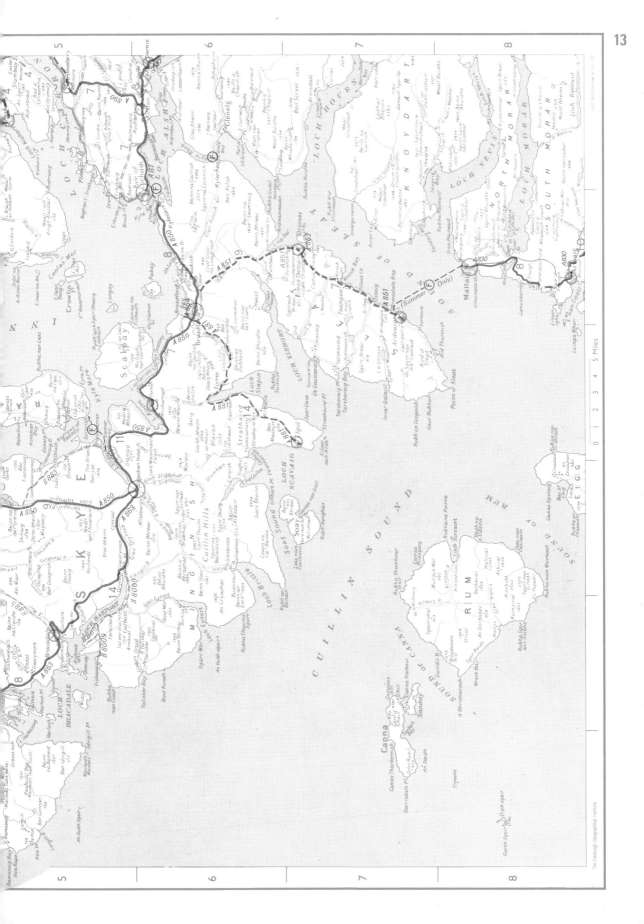

0 1 2 3 4 5 Miles

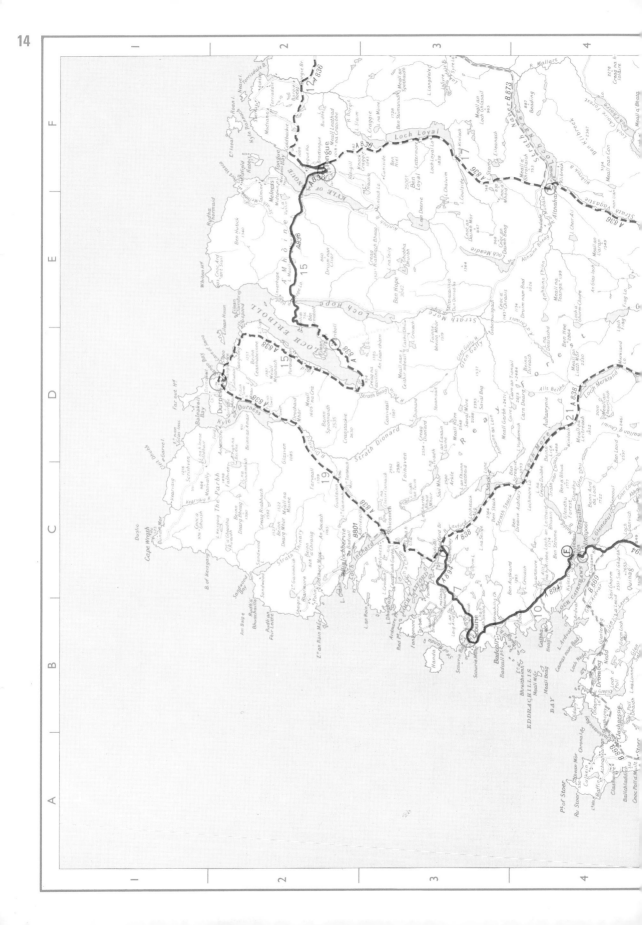